Models of Power

University of Nebraska Press: Lincoln and London

Models of Power

David F. Bell

Politics

and Economics in

Zola's

Rougon-Macquart

Portions of Chapter 2 have previously been published,
in different form, as "Genealogies and Simulacra in
Zola's *Son Excellence Eugène Rougon*," *MLN* 97, no. 4
(1982): 810-26.

The paper in this book meets the minimum require-
ments of American National Standard for Information
Sciences — Permanence of Paper for Printed Library
Materials, ANSI Z39.48-1984.

Library of Congress Cataloging-in-Publication Data
Bell. David F.
Models of power.
Bibliography: p.
Includes Index.
1. Zola, Emile, 1840-1902. Rougon-Macquart.
2. Zola, Emile, 1840-1902 — Political and social
views. 3. Zola, Emile, 1840-1902 — Knowledge —
Economics. 4. Politics in literature. 5. Economics in
literature. I. Title.
PZ2518.B45   1988   843'.8   87-10779
ISBN 0-8032-1201-1 (alkaline paper)

Contents

	vii	ACKNOWLEDGMENTS
	ix	INTRODUCTION
1	1	POLITICAL REPRESENTATION: *SON EXCELLENCE EUGÈNE ROUGON*
2	26	REPRESENTATIONAL STRATEGIES
3	57	DEEDS AND INCEST: *LA CURÉE*
4	96	THE PLAY OF FASHION: *AU BONHEUR DES DAMES*
5	125	TAKING STOCK: *L'ARGENT*
	166	CLOSURE
	173	NOTES
	187	SELECTED BIBLIOGRAPHY
	191	INDEX

Acknowledgments

Josué Harari has been a perspicacious
and untiring reader of my work, and
I would like to take this opportunity
to thank him. My thanks also to
René Girard, who, with his usual insight, read an earlier version of this
essay. Throughout various conversations, Lawrence Schehr and Pierre
Saint-Amand have been both supportive and thought-provoking.

I would like to express my gratitude
to Martine Bell, who has seen this
project through from its inception to
its conclusion and to whom I owe
many a correction.

Introduction

In writing one of his first articles on Balzac, Michel Butor spoke of the myriad of possible roads that lead through *La Comédie humaine*. It does not matter, according to Butor, which road one chooses to follow, provided one is willing to branch out at crossroads and to read enough of the novels so that each new novel studied can begin to add something to what one has already read. Likewise, there are many ways one may enter into Zola's *Les Rougon-Macquart*. Moreover, one quickly discovers that no matter how encompassing a question one might formulate, it is no easy task to cover in any complete manner such a vast corpus. Nor is it perhaps desirable to attempt anything like complete coverage when approaching a work of comparable dimensions. Such a method quickly degenerates into a collection of vague thematic remarks that resemble too closely a series of introductions in some sort of complete edition of the *Rougon-Macquart*. I have therefore deliberately chosen to focus on a specific representative group of novels within Zola's cycle, feeling that by developing my analysis on some very precise points, I could contribute in a more interesting way to the renewed critical appraisal of Zola's work.

The organizing idea around which my reading of the *Rougon-Macquart* has been built is the complex but coherent relationship between political and economic structures in the cycle. Two figures have always fascinated me in the *Rougon-Macquart* series: that of the emperor and that of the speculator. Not that Napoleon III appears with any great regularity in the text of the novels—in many ways his novelistic persona could be subsumed under an analysis akin to Barthes's passing remarks on the place of the historical character in fiction, the "effet de réel," as it were. But an approach of that kind would miss the more subtle functioning of the emperor in such novels as *Son Excellence Eugène Rougon* or *La Débâcle,* where his figure hovers over the text, in the background, ready to make an appearance to lend a sort of legitimacy to certain events and structures. In fact, as I shall argue in the early chapters of the present study, the question of legitimacy becomes a fundamental one in the context of an exploration of the emperor's role in Zola's series. The strategies through which Napoleon III attempts to establish a transcendence capable of legitimizing the power he holds over others will be seen in the context of a logic of the symbolic not limited solely to the political domain, a logic just as clearly identifiable in the economic sphere—that of gold understood as the universal equivalent in the structure of exchange Marx was describing at about the time Zola began publishing the *Rougon-Macquart* series.

The connection between strategies of political power and economic practices led me to reflect more carefully on the meaning of the figure of the speculator as represented in the series by two characters in particular: Aristide Saccard and Octave Mouret. Both seem utterly at home in the context of the Second Empire as it is described by Zola. Both consciously link their enterprises to the rise of the political system created by the second emperor. Saccard does so in a scene at the beginning of *La Curée* during which he looks out over Paris from Montmartre and tries to conceive of the topographical changes to be wrought by Haussmann's undertakings. Mouret ties his ascension to that of the empire in the context of his impassioned defense of his store's expansion, which is to culminate in a grand façade squarely facing one of the city's splendid new boulevards, the Rue du Dix-Décembre. The link between Aristide and Octave on the one hand and Napoleon III on the other goes deeper still. The speculator's constant search for extreme abstraction in his financial operations leads him toward a manipulation of signifiers which is directly related to the activities of the emperor himself. As my argument progresses, it will become apparent that the structure of Second Empire society as Zola conceives it possesses an underlying and encompassing logic that unifies initially distinct domains in a surprisingly tight manner. Even those who attempt to mount some kind of opposition to the practices inherent in the politico-economic structure they confront will find themselves recuperated to a large degree by the very movement they wish to halt or deny.

I certainly do not mean to suggest that Zola's empire possesses an overwhelming monolithic force which sweeps everything before it as it steamrolls across French society. We shall see in the course of the present study that the very characteristics which lend a seemingly undeniable strength to those who exercise political and economic power within the empire of the *Rougon-Macquart* simultaneously produce a fragility which can only lead to a catastrophic collapse. Thus, I shall insist on the fundamental importance not only of *La Débâcle*, the novel which recounts the stunning French defeat at Sedan, but also of *L'Argent*, the novel directly preceding *La Débâcle*, which recounts the story of a disastrous bankruptcy destroying Saccard's Banque Universelle and dragging a myriad of other investors down into poverty and ruin. This pairing of disasters is not haphazard, but is, rather, a significant choice made by Zola in the composition of his novelistic cycle.

Recent theoretical work on the relationship between literature and economic concepts has been important in the formulation of my own argument concerning Zola's work. I would cite Marc Shell in this context, who, since the publication of *The Economy of Literature,* has been exploring the ways in which money and economics have an impact on literature. Among critics of American literature, Walter Benn Michaels has made many thoughtful and pertinent comments on the development of American realism and naturalism during the formative period of American capitalism toward the end of the nineteenth century, remarks which suggest parallels between the American and the French situations during that period. Michaels's study of Theodore Dreiser's portrait of a financial genius, Frank Cowperwood in *The Financier,* reveals a remarkable resemblance between American descriptions of the speculator and those found in Zola's work. In France, Jean-Joseph Goux, beginning with articles published in the late sixties and early seventies and continuing in his recent *Les Monnayeurs du langage,* has explored literature in light of economic structures in a most suggestive manner. His hypothesis linking naturalism to the gold standard and revealing difficulties in the transition toward a monetary system no longer based on gold (difficulties he detects and describes in Gide's *Les Faux Monnayeurs*) merits serious consideration, even though, as it will become clear, my own interpretation of Zola differs from his.

If one must certainly say that with Balzac the economic aspects of French social life make a massive and enduring entrance into the tissue of the novel, one must also say that Zola places himself in that same tradition and brings to the French novel further profound observations on the place and importance of economic structures in the society he describes. With Zola, however, we are already in a different period, one during which the very success of economic mechanisms, their increasingly encompassing nature, has resulted in a paradoxical frailty, a susceptibility to disturbances that seems to menace the very stability without which they could not exist or function. An atmosphere of impending disaster permeates the series (captured marvelously by the image of the unmanned locomotive rushing full tilt into the night at the end of *La Bête humaine*), not only because Zola wrote after the fact and already knew of the debacle he was to describe, but, more fundamentally, because he came to see that debacle as a logical and necessary conclusion to the processes at work within the *Rougon-Macquart*.

1. Political Representation:
Son Excellence Eugène Rougon

Genealogies and Simulacra: Napoleon(s)

The figure of Napoleon III is a suggestive point of departure for an analysis of political structures in *Les Rougon-Macquart*. Zola critics have given a certain amount of attention to the figure of the emperor, but have by no means fully explored the political implications of his character.[1] The absence of a more detailed analysis warrants correction for several reasons. First, the *Rougon-Macquart* represents in many ways a debunking of the Napoleonic myth by a member of the post-Romantic generation of writers in France. For Zola, it is no longer possible to appeal to the glory of the First Empire in order to condemn the Second. But perhaps more important, the depiction of Napoleon III allows Zola to expose some of the mechanisms of political power that possess validity in a more general context largely exceeding the boundaries of the Second Empire. Finally, the destiny of the Rougon-Macquart family itself is structurally related to some of the important elements apparent in Napoleon III's exercise of political power. A key scene from *Son Excellence Eugène Rougon* will furnish us with a starting point for an analysis that will then branch out to follow important developments which carry over into other novels of the series. The contention will be that Zola's portrait of the emperor possesses a logical coherence belying his episodic appearances throughout the

Rougon-Macquart cycle, a coherence which contributes greatly to the cohesion of the society Zola describes in the series.

The fourth chapter of *Son Excellence Eugène Rougon* is a centerpiece of the first part of the novel: there the emperor appears in person for the first time. On the occasion of the baptism of Napoleon's newborn son, there is to be a procession through Paris to Notre Dame. The procession begins at the Quai de l'Horloge, crosses the Seine at the Pont d'Arcole, and continues from there to Notre Dame. At the Pont d'Arcole, "in the opening pierced through the heart of the city by the river, there was room for an entire people."[2] Such is the first purpose of the procession: it is a theatrical spectacle. The populace as a whole has been invited to behold the emperor. The problem, then, is to devise an itinerary along which the greatest number of spectators can be accommodated. Accordingly, the banks of the Seine have been pressed into service along with the large square in front of the Hôtel de Ville: "on both sides of the river, from the Quai Saint-Paul to the Quai de la Mégisserie, from the Quai Napoléon to the Quai de l'Horloge, sidewalks unfolded along wide streets. The Place de l'Hôtel-de-Ville, facing the river, spread forth like a plain. Above these vast spaces, the sky, a warmly pure June sky, capped off the scene with an enormous patch of its infinite blue" (2:85–86). One should not underestimate the logistics involved here. This is not yet a Paris remodeled by Haussmann, and it is no easy task to find the space necessary to organize the emperor's public display.

The success of the setting requires, in addition, the presence of spectators: "Along the sidewalks stood unending lines of curious spectators, squeezed against the railings and walls" (2:86). From a topographical overview the narrator moves to a sociological description of the crowd and passes in review a gamut of classes from the bourgeois down to the lowly laundresses. In all, there are "three to four thousand people" (2:87) amassed in the streets, the windows, and even on the roofs. Up to this point, the narrator gives the impression that he is highlighting diverse details of the scene at random. However, through the device of perspective, he unifies the description by abruptly focusing on the real, but displaced, center of attention of all those gathered along the procession's route:

But something could be seen from all sides—from
the banks of the river, the bridges, the windows:
on the horizon, on the blank wall of a seven-story
building on the Ile Saint-Louis was a giant gray
frock coat, a mural painted in profile with its left
sleeve folded at the elbow, as if this piece of clothing
had kept the shape and fullness of a body which had
disappeared. In the bright sunlight above the teem-
ing mass of onlookers, the monumental advertisement assumed an extraordinary importance. (2:86)

A first reading of the passage leaves one with the impression that
the size and height of this advertisement endow it with a ubiquitous quality and are the sole reasons for its apparent importance.
However, Zola has merely set the stage at this point. The monumental fresco returns in the text at two later moments in the description of the procession, and the second time it is mentioned,
the key to its interpretation is suggested rather directly. When the
carriages of the procession draw fully into view, it is as if they were
framed by the gigantic advertisement.

In the distance above the bridge, serving as a back-
drop to the scene, the monumental advertisement
painted on the wall of the seven-story building on
the Ile Saint-Louis rose up, the giant gray frock
coat, emptied of its body, illuminated by the sun
in a radiant apotheosis.
    Gilquin espied the frock coat as it rose above
the two carriages and shouted:
    "Look! The uncle, over there!" (2:97)

M. and Mme Charbonnel, whom Théodore Gilquin is escorting
during the procession, do not grasp the allusion, but the other
members of the crowd of spectators, as well as the reader, cannot
mistake it. The fresco represents the uncle, the first emperor,
Napoleon I. Suddenly an unimportant detail from the first description of the advertisement—"its left sleeve folded at the elbow"—is invested with significance, replaying the familiar Napoleonic pose with the arm folded across the breast. Aside from its
size, the fresco is monumental because it is literally a *monumentum,*

a reminder of the absent predecessor. Appropriately, that very absence is figured in the monument itself: the frock coat maintains its volume even though the body that would have filled it has now disappeared. Despite his material absence from the scene and from the fresco itself, the first Napoleon is omnipresent.[3] In order to stress this point even further, Zola is not content simply to frame the passing carriages with the fresco; he actually frames the entire narrative sequence in exactly the same way. The first reference to the frock coat comes at the beginning of chapter 4 as Zola sets the scene of the procession's itinerary, and the chapter closes with the third and final mention of the huge mural:

> And in the light mist which was rising from the Seine, over there, at the tip of the Ile Saint-Louis, the only thing one could distinguish among the blurred gray façades was the giant frock coat, the monumental advertisement, as if hung upon a hook on the horizon, the cast-off, bourgeois clothing of some titan whose limbs had been dissolved by lightning. (2:109)

The presence of the first emperor is overwhelming enough in the form of a gigantic advertisement, but this is not the last time the reader is reminded of him as the festivities described in chapter 4 unfold. The procession arrives at the cathedral, where the invited dignitaries enter for the continuation of the ceremony while everyone else remains outside. Mme Correur, however, persists in her attempt to penetrate into the inner sanctum. She is unsuccessful, but she does catch a glimpse of the interior of Notre Dame through the open doors. The descriptive device of presenting a scene through the eyes of a spectator provides the means for Zola to give an account of the proceedings.[4] He does so with brio in a passage of the text that culminates in an extremely significant fashion: "In the midst of a tremendous cheer which made the vaults tremble, Mme Correur saw the emperor standing on the edge of the platform above the crowd. He was set off in black against the flaming gold of the candles which the bishops were lighting behind him. He was showing the imperial prince to the people, a ball of white lace held very high in his two upraised arms" (2:102). The description alludes in unmistakable terms to another scene in Notre Dame in which someone else raised his hands above his head—not to display a child, but to display a crown. The reference, of course, is to Napoleon I's coronation. Although there is no direct mention of the uncle in this particular passage, Zola has manifestly telescoped together two similar scenes. The superimposition invites the reader to explore the relationship between the two Napoleons as it develops in chapter 4 of *Son Excellence Eugène Rougon*.

What is the meaning of Napoleon III's gesture of raising his son into everyone's view? First and most obviously, the spectators are witnessing the reaffirmation of a dynasty. The son is the successor, and his baptism before the Empire assembled signifies his entry into legitimacy. The son's legitimacy simultaneously implies and rests on that of the father. Rather than focusing upon the events of 2 December 1851 and 2 December 1852, Zola approaches the question of legitimacy by emphasizing the supremely charged baptismal moment. Napoleon III skirts the issue of his self-proclamation as emperor in the founding of the Second Empire and instead claims his right to the throne by inserting himself into a lineage that reaches beyond him. The question of lineage is indeed central here. Is Napoleon III a *true* pretender, an inheritor of the legacy of his illustrious uncle, or, on the contrary, a *false* pretender, a simulacrum of the Napoleonic myth?

Those of Zola's contemporaries who were opposed to Napoleon III were inclined to criticize the emperor by comparing him to his predecessor, thereby drawing the conclusion that he was at best a pale replica. However, the stance adopted by one who condemns Napoleon III by reference to the glory of his uncle contains a hidden danger. Such an approach implicitly amounts to granting legitimacy to Napoleon III. By glorifying Napoleon I's reign as a model with respect to which a later emperor may fall short, one accepts the legitimacy of the original emperor. One therefore tacitly allows the lineage established by Napoleon I to endure by granting it the right to continue in unbroken fashion. There may be greater or lesser members of that dynasty, but its existence has nevertheless been accepted as a fact. Thus although many critics of Napoleon III wished to convict him as a false pretender, in essence their arguments transformed him into a true pretender.

The perspicacity of the approach adopted by Zola in chapter 4 of *Son Excellence Eugène Rougon* now becomes clearer. By superimposing Napoleon III's gesture of raising his child above his head upon that of Napoleon I's raising of the crown of his coronation, Zola underscores the utter absence of foundation from the very beginning of the dynasty. Napoleon I's self-crowning is a denial of origin, of foundation, a symbolic denial of the father and therefore of genealogy.[5] By interrupting the line of kings, he subverts the model but at the same time institutes himself as model: he subverts and destroys the genealogical hierarchy implicit in the concept of kingliness. Napoleon III's appeal to the lineage of his predecessor, then, refers back to a foundation that the predecessor, Napoleon I, rejected in his own inaugural gesture. Only if one refuses to consider the full ramifications of Napoleon I's self-coronation can one fall into the trap of measuring Napoleon III against his uncle. Once one falls into that trap, however, no amount of criticism directed against Napoleon III can impugn the legitimacy of lineage one has indirectly and almost inadvertently conceded him. Zola's subtle reference to the self-coronation points out the problematic nature of Napoleon I's gesture and subsequently permits the novelist to question the legitimacy of Napoleon III in a much more profound manner.

The self-coronation is indeed a fascinating gesture that reveals in Napoleon I a curious parallel with the working of the simulacrum, at least as Gilles Deleuze and others have interpreted the idea of the simulacrum in Plato's work. What is a simulacrum? Platonic doctrine deals in a specific manner with the problem of the relationship between an original model (an idea) and its copies. There are essentially two types of imitation, two types of copies: the good or correct one and the simulacrum. As Vincent Descombes puts it, "An image resembles the original if simultaneously it somehow illustrates that model and yet indicates that there is a model of which it, as image, is only a copy. . . . But there is another type of imitation, the simulacrum . . . which pretends to a different type of resemblance: to be so similar to the original that the beholder can no longer distinguish between the two."[6] In other words, imitation is governed by a hierarchy over which reigns the original to which all copies are subordinated. Into this harmonious system the simulacrum introduces a perversion: its resemblance disrupts the hierarchy and in fact threatens to turn it upside down, because the simulacrum attempts to assume the position of a model. Gilles Deleuze remarks, "Copies are possessors who are second in line, well-founded pretenders, guaranteed by their resemblance; *simulacra* are like false pretenders, built on the principle of dissimilarity, implying an essential perversion or misappropriation." Deleuze pictures the Platonic method of distinction and division not as a simple means of arriving at definitions and proper classifications, but as "a dialectic of rivalry . . . a dialectic of rivals or pretenders." He continues by defining the aim of Platonism as follows: "At the heart of the matter is the attempt to assure the triumph of copies over simulacra, to repress simulacra, to keep them imprisoned in the depths, to prevent them from rising to the surface and permeating everything."[7] Accordingly, to overthrow Platonism would require a strategic intervention to undo the authoritative relation between model and copy: "To deny the primacy of an original over its copy, of a model over its image. To glorify the reign of simulacra and reflections."[8]

The self-coronation of Napoleon I is a gesture that is linked to the workings of the simulacrum. By his self-investiture, the first Napoleon breaks the hierarchy of the kingly lineage and negates the model, but at the same time he sets himself up as more kingly than the king he is replacing. With this "original" act in mind, one may grasp more clearly the fundamentally flawed nature of Napoleon III's gesture. His reign is doubly unfounded: first because he attempts to base it on an idea of lineage that was undone earlier by his uncle, and secondly because his reign amounts to a willful confusion between himself and his predecessor, although the predecessor's coronation act had already revealed that recourse to him as model was profoundly problematic. Ultimately, this passage of *Son Excellence* suggestively outlines one type of political strategy that characterizes the Second Empire as viewed by Zola:

the Empire is a reign of illusion, substitution, appearances, reflections, and masks. Dissimulation of origins with a view to political and social manipulation is a widespread and regular phenomenon, as we shall see.

Although Zola was no reader of Marx, and vice versa, the treatments of Napoleon III that one finds in their respective works show some interesting similarities. A few brief remarks concerning the Marxist theory of the state within the context of Marx's *The Eighteenth Brumaire of Louis Bonaparte* will serve to bring out points of agreement. In one of its main thrusts, Marx's political analysis of the state attempts to expose the fictitious content of the idealistic notion according to which the state is viewed as the representative of the nation as a whole. For Marx, the organs of the state would represent instead the class or classes that dominate a given society. This principle of analysis is applied in *The Eighteenth Brumaire,* in which Marx explores the conflicting interests of the various Second Republic parliamentary groups and demonstrates the connection between those interests and the interests of various social and economic milieus that the parliamentary parties represented. However, within the context of such an analysis, Bonapartism can only be seen as the eruption of a scandal that seriously undermines this newly revised notion of the representativity of the state. In fact, it marks "the emergence of a State which has been emptied of its class content."[9] The only possible class content that one could assign to Bonapartism would be that of the small peasantry. This is what Marx argues at the beginning of *The Eighteenth Brumaire.* The election of Louis Bonaparte to the presidency on 10 December 1848 "was a *reaction of the peasants,* who had to pay the costs of the February revolution, against the other classes of the nation, a *reaction of the country against the town.*" Yet Marx is forced to admit that less than two years later, "the peasants had been disappointed in all their hopes; they were oppressed more than ever."[10] As Jeffrey Mehlman puts it, "In relation to the peasantry, Bonapartism offers only a semblance of representation."[11] To consolidate his position, Bonaparte resorts to the strategy of playing the various groups off against one another constantly, of entering into momentary alliances that he dissolves when it becomes expedient to do so. In a fundamental sense, he really represents the interest of no single group or groups with any degree of permanence.

This antagonism between state and society produces a break within the category of representation, both in a political and in a wider philosophical sense. Into the specular relationship between the instance of political power and its constituency—that is, between the state and the dominant class or classes—a political entity is introduced, one which subverts the representative tie. This subversion is comparable to the one accomplished by the simulacrum when it undoes the relationship between a model and its copy. The resonances of the structures of legitimacy analyzed in Zola's *Son Excellence* are unmistakable here. For although Zola does not cast the problem in terms of parties and constituencies (at least not in the passage we have been analyzing), the relation between model and copy at the heart of the baptismal scene is structurally equivalent to that explored by Marx in his analysis of parties and constituencies. Moreover, as in the case of Zola, these reflections lead Marx to see Napoleon I in a new light in which his once-accepted greatness is questioned. Marx writes to Engels in 1858, "In point of fact, he [Napoleon III] is not only Napoléon le Petit, in Victor Hugo's sense, that is, the antithesis of Napoléon le Grand: he personifies even more, and quite marvelously, the pettiness of the great Napoleon."[12] The idea of pettiness leads directly back to the giant mural with which the present analysis began. The fact that Zola chooses to use a clothing advertisement as the representation of Napoleon I in the procession scene is not without significance. Nothing could seem less noble or more bourgeois than a clothing advertisement. The "monument" to Napoleon III's predecessor is calculated immediately to deny Napoleon I any noble or heroic dimension. At the very heart of the supposed grandeur of the first emperor lurks a bourgeois pettiness. Zola is not content simply to imply the idea: he expresses it clearly in the telling phrase that closes chapter 4 of *Son Excellence Eugène Rougon*. The gigantic suit of clothes is presented as "the cast-off, bourgeois clothing of some titan" (2:109).

The procession scene in *Son Excellence* contains further confirmation of the hypothesis that the simulacrum is a pervasive dimension of Zola's Second Empire. This confirmation appears in the form of a narrative undertaken by Théodore Gilquin. The reader will recall that it is Gilquin who links the gigantic fresco (the center of everyone's attention at a critical moment of the procession scene) and the uncle. Later he has a second occasion to function as a mediating figure. As the carriages of the baptismal procession come into view and then pass in front of him and his party, composed of the Charbonnels and Mme Correur, he notices Eugène Rougon, the recently dismissed minister of Napoleon III's government. Rougon in turn espies Gilquin and then tries to avoid his gaze: "Rougon, whose senator's garb made him a center of attention, sank back quickly into the recesses of the carriage" (2:92). Gilquin subsequently experiences a moment of bitterness at the lack of recognition for his role in bringing about the empire, a bitterness that he expresses by narrating the mysterious beginnings of Rougon's career. Since Rougon's beginnings and those of the empire itself coincide, the reader is afforded a swift glimpse of the political activities surrounding the establishment of the empire, one of the few such revelations provided in the *Rougon-Macquart* series. Gilquin, who previously worked with Rougon, explains that he was responsible for winning over elements of the Parisian proletariat to the Bonapartist cause. "At this point Gilquin lowered his voice a little and blinked his eyes expressively, because, after all, he too had been a member of Rougon's band. He was in charge of covering the low-class bars on the outskirts of the city, where he would shout, 'Vive la République!' Well, you had to be a republican in order to recruit followers" (2:94). The goal of the early Bonapartist movement was to mime republicanism so closely that, in the eyes of the dangerous classes (the proletariat), Napoleon and the republic appeared synonymous. The only way to immobilize the opposition that could be mounted by the working-class against the Bonapartist cause was for that cause to create a simulacrum, to appear so much like the republican movement that it was impossible to distinguish between the two. Thus the role of Gilquin and others like him was to create a base of working-class support by speaking the language of republicanism. Only when the coup d'état was complete, only when the simulacrum had worked its confusion and subversion, were the differences between republicanism and Bonapartism allowed to become manifest. The spectators were duped, in other words, by a willfully pretended false appearance. Small wonder that Rougon fears Gilquin enough to hide in the back of the carriage: Gilquin possesses the secret of the unresolved paradox concerning the foundation of the regime. Even Gilquin himself realizes the enormous effect that the rendering explicit of the simulacrum might have, and instinctively moves to protect his secret at the very moment when he reveals it: "At this point, Gilquin lowered his voice a little."

This reversal of republic into empire is so vital to Zola's depiction of the Second Empire that it is played out a second time in a crucial scene found in *La Fortune des Rougon*. I am referring to the capture of the Plassans city hall by republican forces headed by Antoine Macquart and its subsequent recapture by Bonapartist loyalists headed by Pierre Rougon. All the various ramifications of this episode are interesting, but for the moment I should like to focus on one significant detail. The republican column that passes through Plassans seeking to join battle with the Bonapartist forces actually meets no resistance and simply occupies the empty city hall and mayor's office. The column's passage is quite swift; left behind afterwards is a small detachment headed by Antoine Macquart in charge of assuring the occupation of the city offices. Macquart's first order of business as head of the revolutionary forces is to write a proclamation destined to be posted throughout Plassans. The text of that proclamation is as follows: "Residents of Plassans, the hour of independence has struck, the reign of justice has arrived" (1:226). However, precisely at the moment when one of the republicans is reading the final version aloud, Pierre Rougon and his Bonapartist partisans burst into the mayor's office and subdue the republicans. In what appears to be almost a retake of the preceding scene, the first action of the new masters of the mayor's office is to compose their own proclamation: "Roudier declared that before doing anything else it would be a good idea to address a proclamation to the town residents" (1:229). This is the first in a series of significant acts through which a symmetry between the two supposedly opposing groups is established. Moreover, it is not even necessary to devise a totally new proclamation. "In fact, Pierre was reading the one which the insurrectionists had left on the table. 'But,' he exclaimed, 'this fits our purposes perfectly. There are only a few words to be changed' " (1:229). The new proclamation reads thus: "Residents of Plassans, the hour of resistance has struck, the reign of order has returned" (1:230). Republic and empire are amalgamated to such a degree that it is not even necessary to introduce a fundamental alteration of rhetorical structure in order to pass from one to the other: a word changed here or there will suffice. Further, Antoine and Pierre do not differ from one another in any overriding ideological sense. Each has established a political base aimed simply at personal aggrandizement. The goal of each brother is perfectly comparable to that of the other: to use the political situation for private advantage. In other words, the two are essentially twins, and they could trade sides without fundamentally affecting their mutual rivalry. The opposition republic/empire is superseded by a more encompassing identity that can only confuse the issue of political difference between republic and empire. Once again the foundation of the Second Empire lacks the certainty of any clear-cut political distinctions: these distinctions are mere appearances, simulacra designed to obscure the usurpation that is actually taking place.[13]

The question of usurpation and blurred differences with respect to the two brothers, Antoine and Pierre, is directly related to the problem of the foundations of the Rougon-Macquart family itself. The history of the family during the Second Empire is largely the result of an original usurpation of which the scene in the Plassans city hall described above is a repetition on the political level. As the title of Zola's series of novels suggests, *Les Rougon-Macquart* recounts the history of a family containing two distinct branches. The dichotomy at stake in the separation of the two branches is a genealogical one resting on the question of legitimacy and illegitimacy. Pierre Rougon is the legitimate fruit of Adélaïde Fouque's short-lived marriage with "a man named Rougon" (1:41). Following Rougon's sudden death, Adélaïde begins an unsanctioned liaison with "Macquart the beggar" (1:42), smuggler and poacher *par excellence,* to whom she bears two bastards, Antoine and Ursule.

Pierre, therefore, is seemingly the rightful heir, being the only child of the legitimate side of the family's lineage. Yet from the very beginning, that legitimacy is questionable, at least in the eyes of the other members of the Plassans community, for they cannot explain Adélaïde's marriage to Rougon, a man so obviously below her in a social sense. "The marriage was a first surprise for public opinion; no one could understand why Adélaïde preferred this poor devil [Rougon], fat, heavy, mediocre, who could hardly speak French, to certain other young men, the sons of wealthy farmers, who had been courting her for a long time" (1:41). Their first explanation is that an extramarital pregnancy forced the marriage, but Pierre's birth a full twelve months later destroys that theory.

Provincial gossip finally discovers an unquenchable source upon which to draw when Adélaïde becomes Macquart's lover. Pierre realizes as he grows older that, despite his own genealogical legitimacy, his situation as a respectable member of the Plassans community will always be in jeopardy simply because of his contact with the unconventionality of his mother's behavior as well as with the illegitimacy of his half-brother and half-sister. He hits upon a solution: although he is not legally the full inheritor of his mother's property, he schemes to cheat his half-brother and half-sister by stealing their share. In seizing full control of the family assets, Pierre hopes to solidify his position as the sole legitimate representative of the family. Thus, usurpation supplements and strengthens genealogical legitimacy: the two must coincide if Pierre hopes to be successful.

A similar coincidence of usurpation accompanied by an appeal to genealogical legitimacy is evident in the case of Napoleon III and allows one to put the particular history of the Rougon-Macquart family into a larger perspective. One might say that the Bonapartist usurpation that Zola so masterfully pinpoints in chapter 4 of *Son Excellence Eugène Rougon* is played out on all levels down to the family itself. The reversal of legitimacy into illegitimacy is everywhere threatening. However, by enlisting the forces of ruse and of the simulacrum, the figures in power in the *Rougon-Macquart* succeed in forestalling potentially disastrous discoveries—at least temporarily.

The problem of the simulacrum in the context of political representation raises some wider theoretical questions that merit further consideration. As the earlier reference to Marx and *The Eighteenth Brumaire* suggested, Napoleon III's political power is linked to his ability to assume convincingly in the eyes of the beholder various positions from which he seems to represent different interest groups.[14] He is a republican for the republicans, a protector of the working class for the workers (the projects aimed at the elimination of pauperism), a defender of the interest of small retailers (Lisa Macquart in *Le Ventre de Paris,* for example, constantly refers to the fact that the Second Empire is good for business), a liberal when necessary (the evolution toward the liberal empire is evident at the end of *Son Excellence Eugène Rougon*), and so forth, as far as one wishes to go. The emperor, then, is capable of assuming every position in turn; he is a figure of constant substitution, standing for everything and (at the same time) for nothing in particular.

When one grasps the function of Napoleon III within the political sphere, one begins to see some striking homologies between his role and that of gold as money within the sphere of economic exchange. As Jean-Joseph Goux has argued, "The genesis of the money form is theoretically homologous to the genesis of political *representation*."[15] A discussion of Marx's theory of the origin of money in the realm of exchange would permit us to develop this parallel in a more detailed manner. Goux's *Freud, Marx: Economie et symbolique* provides a succinct and perceptive summary and interpretation of that theory, and I shall borrow from his account in my exposition.[16]

According to Marx, the development of money in economic exchange is a process that can be broken down into four distinct phases. The first phase, the simple or accidental form of value, is characterized by a simple equation: "The first commodity's value character emerges here through its own relation to the second commodity."[17] In this, the original equation and point of departure, two commodities enter into a specular relationship: "The physical body of commodity B becomes a mirror for the value of commodity A" (*Capital,* 1:144). The second commodity, serving as equivalent in the equation, does not express its own value, but functions rather as a material support for the expression of the first commodity's relative value. This first equivalence contains the germ of what later becomes monetary exchange, but it must first undergo a series of transformations.

The second phase in the genesis of money is the total or expanded form of value. Marx describes this form as follows: "The value of the commodity, the linen for example, is now expressed in terms of innumerable other members of the world of commodities. Every other physical commodity now becomes a mirror of the linen's value" (*Capital,* 1:155). However, this second phase is unsatisfactory for two essential reasons. First, the exchange value of the single commodity whose relative value one is attempting to establish "can . . . be exhaustively expressed only by the infinite number of equations in which the use-values of all other commodities form its equivalent. The only exhaustive expression for a *universal equivalent* is the sum of these equations or the totality of the different proportions in which a commodity can be exchanged for any other commodity. . . . This is in fact an infinite series."[18] Secondly, if one takes the problem from the point of view of the commodities that are functioning as equivalents to the commodity whose relative value one is seeking to establish, "each type of equivalent commodity is enmeshed in other relationships in which it is itself the relative form of an infinite number of equivalents" (Goux, *Freud, Marx,* p. 59). Thus one is left with a conflicting network of value expressions, a situation of rivalry and relativism from which it is impossible to escape if one remains at this level. As Marx comments, one has at this stage "a motley mosaic of disparate and unconnected expressions of value" (*Capital,* 1:156).

To find a solution to the problem, one must move to the third phase of the genesis of money, the general form of value. At this point, all the multiple relations between commodities are reduced to a single common denominator. All commodities now express their relative exchange values through one commodity considered as universal or general equivalent. One thus eliminates the series of conflicting value expressions and simplifies not only the expression of the value of any single commodity, but also the expression of the relation of that commodity to all others. The accession of the exchange process to this third phase really represents the normalization of social relations in the form of a universal circuit of economic exchanges. Finally, the culmination of the genesis of monetary exchange occurs in the fourth phase of development, the money form itself. The entire group of commodities converges toward the unique universal equivalent, which is historically gold. Gold then functions as money, the central equivalent that measures the value of commodities in simplified equations.

Let us examine for a moment the general principles involved in the process just described. The fundamental driving force behind the development of the monetary value form is the distinction between the use value and the exchange value of a commodity:

> While the *use value* is determined solely by the properties belonging to the object which is the commodity, in other words, by the empirical thing as physical support with the various and accidental qualities inherent to its corporality, the *exchange value,* on the contrary, expresses a more substantial and permanent foundation: the identity, the thing itself, the universal. The exchange value is founded upon the disappearance of every empirical determination.
> (Goux, *Freud, Marx,* p. 63)

In the process of exchange, the sensual aspects of the commodity are sublimated in order to expose the suprasensual, invisible, supernatural abstraction that permits commodities to be viewed from the perspective of their essential identity. Moreover, this spiritualistic opposition between body and soul is parallel to an idealistic opposition between idea and reality. Marx is clear on this point:

> In order to equate [the commodity] with itself as an exchange value, it is exchanged for a symbol which represents it as exchange value as such. As such a symbolized exchange value, it can then in turn be exchanged in definite relations for every other com-

modity. Because the product becomes a commodity, and the commodity becomes an exchange value, it obtains, at first only in the head, a double existence. This doubling in the idea proceeds (and must proceed) to the point where the commodity appears double in real exchange: as a natural product on one side, as exchange value on the other. I.e. the commodity's exchange value obtains a material existence separate from the commodity. [19]

The exchange value of a commodity appears as an idea, a symbol, in opposition to its concrete reality, its use value. What begins as an idea, however, ultimately finds material expression, as the passage quoted from Marx suggests. The exchange value, which is first considered as abstract and symbolic, is, in the final stage of development, embodied in gold as money which has an actual material existence separate from the commodity.

Herein lies the aura of sovereignty that is attached to gold as universal equivalent. As embodiment of an idea, an abstraction, it functions almost as a transcendental concept, something given from without the system of commodities that it governs. In the process of transformation whereby all other commodities converge upon it as the general equivalent, it is progressively excluded from the realm of mere commodities. Marx comments: "The commodity that figures as universal equivalent is . . . excluded from the uniform and therefore universal relative form of value" (*Capital*, 1:161). Gold is set opposite commodities and becomes the absolute arbiter of their value, arbiter sent from another world, as it were. The exclusion of gold from the realm of mere commodities endows it with a transcendental character that ultimately veils the whole process of the genesis of monetary exchange and presents gold as a mediator that has always been given. Marx captures this quality when he calls gold "the god of commodities."[20]

In fact, gold as money can occupy a position of transcendence only if the genesis of the monetary form through four distinct phases is obscured or forgotten. Gold itself was originally a mere commodity, and only if that fact is neglected can its position of prestige and uniqueness be maintained. "The movement through which

Political Representation

this process has been mediated vanishes in its own result, leaving no trace behind" (*Capital*, 1:187). By analyzing the genesis of money, Marx offers an explanation of the valorization of gold that is characteristic of a market economy, a valorization that the obscured genesis of the monetary form renders possible. But he does more: he reveals the development of a *process of symbolization* whereby one element is set off from a system and becomes capable of standing for other elements in the system.

The contention is that this process of symbolization possesses a wider and more general pertinence than is immediately apparent. Interpreting the genesis of the money form in a strictly economic sense is insufficient. One need only peruse Marx's prefaces to the first and second editions of *Capital* to realize the importance he attributed to the first section of *Capital* and the care he took in rewriting and improving it. The exposition of the development of the money form contains numerous asides and allusions to more general questions—in the multiple spheres of social organization—opened up by Marx's analysis. As Goux states:

> A scientific system of "metaphors" exists, a methodical working out of equivalences and substitutions *across* distant domains of the general social body. We are speaking principally here of none other than the axis of the *paternal metaphor* (money, phallus, language, monarch), the central and centralizing metaphor which permits all the others to be anchored, the pivot of all symbolic legislation, the locus of the standard [*étalon*] (from the word *estel*: stake, pole) and of oneness. (*Freud, Marx*, p. 65)

Goux's point is that a remarkable isomorphism exists between the genesis of money and the genesis of other fundamental centralizing symbols of capitalist society—father, phallus, monarch (although I find Goux's use of the word "scientifique" rather puzzling here).

It is now possible to understand more fully the function of Napoleon III in Zola's description of the Second Empire and to develop the insight according to which the genesis of the money form is isomorphic to the development of political representation. Within the context of Marx's treatment of the emperor in *The Eighteenth Brumaire,* Napoleon III appeared to be an aberration because he failed to represent any constituency with a modicum of permanence. However, if one views the problem from the more general theoretical level outlined above, Napoleon III's function in the structure of political representation is perhaps not as flawed 19 as it might first appear. Precisely because he cannot be identified with any one specific constituency, he can set himself opposite all groups in the position of general equivalent. Standing above the various ideologies that exist in the political sphere, he is thus an arbiter, free to support or to abandon any position at will. He provides a point of exchange for the various ideologies that vie for supremacy under his regime. Differences that distinguish various political groups, whatever they may be, are effaced through his mediation: they become equivalent.

The *Rougon-Macquart* series does not furnish the reader with the means of following the genesis of the emperor's power as a whole process. Jean Borie has commented quite accurately on the ex-centric and marginal nature of the presentation of the Second Empire by Zola.[21] Indeed, the reader of the *Rougon-Macquart* has little sense of the becoming of the second emperor's political regime; it is almost as if Zola's empire were without roots in what preceded it. By the time Zola finally brings the reader to Paris in *La Curée,* the coup d'état is so far removed that the birth of the Second Empire seems the result of an immaculate conception: "The tribune as well as the newspapers had fallen silent. Society, saved once again, was congratulating itself, resting, sleeping late now that a strong government was protecting it and relieving it even of the bother of thinking and taking care of its own affairs" (1:367). This is to be expected, however, and is perhaps less paradoxical than Borie suggests. We have seen that the transcendental position of the general equivalent depends to a great extent on the fact that its origin is obscured in the very process of its development. The structure of Zola's series accurately renders this fact.

Concerning the rise of Napoleon III, however, Zola's text does furnish some suggestive elements to the perspicacious reader. In particular, one must recall the confusion between republicanism and Bonapartism that is visible in the work of Gilquin during his propaganda forays into outlying Parisian cafés and that is also evident in the confrontation between Antoine Macquart and Pierre Rougon in the Plassans town hall. In both cases, two conflicting series of ideologies confront one another and appear essentially interchangeable. Likewise, two (or more) conflicting networks of value expressions clash in what Marx calls the total or expanded form of value, no one network demonstrating clear superiority over or even difference from the other. The resolution of such conflicts is in both cases the formulation of a third term, gold, which can give an "impartial" value to the two networks of value expressions, or, in the political arena, Napoleon III as dictator, whose emergence quiets warring ideologies and creates a program which allows their cohabitation without conflict (or, at least, with a good deal less conflict).

The vocabulary of confrontation and conflict was intentionally pressed into service in the preceding remarks. Conflict is not the privilege of the political domain alone: one encounters it in the economic domain as well. It is important to point out that the genesis of money is not a purely technical economic process nor is it a smooth, rational development of innate social instincts. On the contrary, the genesis of money can be viewed as the culmination of violent confrontations among exchanging parties. In a recent analysis of the money form, Michel Aglietta and André Orléan argue precisely that economic theory must not take as its starting point the idea that human beings possess an innate disposition toward organized, non-violent exchange. The exchange relation should be seen instead as the result of a fundamental acquisitive violence: "Thus the presupposition retained here is that buying and selling relations are defined by an acquisitive violence, diverted toward objects, which we shall call the *attempt to corner the market*."[22] Once this point of view is adopted, the various stages of the genesis of money become parts of a process during which the violent rivalry between exchanging parties is ended through the engendering of a third term that mediates between the two initial protagonists. That third term is money as a social institution. "Thus the process of socialization engenders a reality which is radically different from the original and primordial rivalry."[23]

Although the genesis of money does introduce a certain stability, it does not altogether eradicate the conflictual nature of exchange relations. Beneath stability always lies the founding violence that is the motor of the exchange system. Thus despite the fact that we live in a relatively well-regulated society based on exchange, we periodically experience moments of economic crisis and inflation which once again induce frenetic behavior on the part of exchanging parties and remind us of the delicate balance that exists between stable exchange and chaos. These reflections suggest the conclusion that the isomorphism between economic and political domains discussed above is perhaps even more detailed than is at first apparent. Confrontations on the economic front contain as much potential for violence as those on the political front. And the threat that the usurper will be overturned is paralleled by the possibility for crisis in the economic sphere during which money is no longer capable of retaining the confidence of those involved in the system of exchange. One can begin here to sense the close relationship between the two novels which fall at the end of the *Rougon-Macquart* series just before *Le Docteur Pascal,* namely, *L'Argent* and *La Débâcle.*

The logic of symbolicity embodied in the genesis of money also provides a means for further understanding the baptismal scene viewed by Mme Correur in Notre Dame. The cathedral itself is the symbolic dwelling of that greatest of transcendentals, God himself. The emperor attempts to affirm his own transcendental stature by associating himself with a center of religious power, the altar of the great cathedral. Moreover, Napoleon III's appeal to the lineage of his uncle is one more attempt to set himself off, to present himself as one whose presence at the center is given from the outside and who therefore stands above the warp and woof of everyday political struggles. One must always bear in mind that fetichization, the process by which a thing takes on the appearance of a given beyond the forces of social production, is a process of obscuring origins. "The fetishism (of gold, the phallus, the monarch) originates in the *erasure of a genesis*" (Goux, *Freud, Marx,* p.

79). Gold as universal equivalent is no longer a mere commodity among others; it is, rather, a mystical cipher through which the value—and meaning—of all commodities can be expressed. By bringing the biological imperative to the forefront, Napoleon III in fact draws a veil over the whole bloody struggle from which he emerged victorious, the struggle through which he attained his position as representative of the various factions on the political scene. The baptismal scene is to be interpreted as the apotheosis of the biological to the detriment of the political.

The procession scene in chapter 4 of *Son Excellence Eugène Rougon,* upon which my analysis has focused thus far, contains an interesting series of confirmations in the thematic register of the structural isomorphism that has been developed up to this point. The first appearance of the emperor in the scene is particularly striking. Gilquin and his party (the Charbonnels and Mme Correur), who are awaiting the arrival of the imperial couple, finally glimpse the imperial carriages as they come into view in the middle of the Pont d'Arcole. The description of the appearance of the carriages culminates in the following passage: "The carriages were advancing slowly, noiselessly. The carriage apron was so airy, with its lazy curves, that the carriages seemed to be suspended above the vast emptiness of the river. Below, on the blue expanse of the water, one could see their reflection, like a strange goldfish swimming just beneath the surface" (2:97). The apparition of the imperial actors upon the stage of the baptismal procession is marked by a golden reflection in the waters of the Seine. This specular description of the emperor's party recalls the mirroring of commodities that gives rise to equivalence and exchange and refers as well to the confusion of reflections bound up in the working of the simulacrum. However, perhaps more important, it is not by chance that the emperor first appears in the middle of a bridge, floating effortlessly between the two banks of the river. The bridge figures quite tellingly the mediating position of Napoleon III as general equivalent in the political realm. His is the power to connect and to be exchanged from one side to the other, between law (the Quai de l'Horloge) and government (the Hôtel de Ville), between government and church (Notre Dame), in an endless movement of circulation symbolically played out in the procession scene.

Shortly before Gilquin espies the emperor's carriage gliding across the Pont d'Arcole, he mentions another detail connected to the baptismal festivities, an element that can take on its full importance only in light of the questions raised by the preceding analysis of political representation in relation to the genesis of the laws of exchange. The procession has furnished the occasion for the striking of a commemorative medallion:

> Finally, [Gilquin] furnished them with a description
> of the one hundred twenty thousand commemorative
> medallions which had been distributed to students,
> to children in primary school and in public asylums,
> to noncommissioned officers and soldiers in the Paris
> army. He even had one himself, and he showed it to
> them. The medallion was the size of a ten-*sous* coin.
> On one side, it contained the profiles of the emperor
> and the empress, on the other the profile of the im-
> perial prince, with the date of baptism: 14 June
> 1856. (2:19)

This is the traditional medallion format: the portrait of the ruler on one side (I shall return to the presence of the empress shortly) and the representation of the event being commemorated with an inscription giving the date on the reverse side. The suggestive point here is the relationship between money and medallion and thus the contribution of the medallion to the problematic of political representation.

What is the relationship between a coin and political power? Louis Marin offers a thoughtful response in a discussion treating related problems:

> In the case of the coin, with both its front and its
> back, a reciprocal guarantee is underwritten: the fig-
> ure of the prince and his name, the image of royal
> authority of which one of the essential signs of sover-
> eignty is the right to strike coins (precisely to en-
> grave his figure and his name upon a coin made of a
> precious metal), this effigy and this name guarantee
> its permanent value. That value is signified on the

back of the coin by certain marks, always identically
reproduced, which authorize its use and its value by
defining a rule of constant exchange among the subjects of the prince.[24]

The ruler, then, is the only one who possesses the right to strike
coins and to establish their value throughout his realm. The coin
represents his ability to force the exchange of goods to pass almost
literally through his person (his effigy is struck on the face of the
coin itself). It functions as a crystallization of his position outside
the group of his subjects: only he can strike coins, while his subjects are reduced to equality before the value enforced by his mint.
Thus his own transcendental aura is, in fact, inscribed upon the
very object that is the center of the process of fetichization contained in the logic of the laws of exchange.

The medallion in turn is related to the coin. In a sense, it also
contains a universal, recognized value, but the content of that value has changed. What is found on the side opposite the portrait
of the ruler is no longer a sign that identifies a monetary value,
but rather the inscription of a singular historical event, presented,
nonetheless, in a form perfectly symmetrical to the money form.
The recognition of the sovereign authority of the ruler implied by
and embodied in the coin is enlisted into the service of the historical event portrayed upon the medallion:

The inscription of the historical event as a representation on the back of the medallion, to the extent
that it is and can only be the miraculous act of the
king, will have the same validity and will receive
the same recognition as the coins marked by the die
of sovereign authority. That authority alone has the
right to produce such marks precisely because it is
sovereign. Such objects designate the sovereignty of
the sovereign by the very fact that only he can mark
them. [25]

The transcendence of the baptized son is reinforced by the fetichism attached to the coin. Moreover, the biological imperative that
is the very point of the baptismal celebration is figured fully on

the medallion, since the portrait of the emperor is replaced by a double inscription: both husband and wife. Indeed, the result is a family portrait: father and mother on one side, son on the reverse side. Ultimately, the medallion is suspended between two symbolic series—political authority on the one hand, the aura of the general equivalent on the other. It bridges those two series and suggestively illustrates their imbrication, while simultaneously recalling the appeal to legitimacy through genealogy at the heart of *Son Excellence Eugène Rougon*.

2. Representational Strategies

Masks and Potentiality: *La Débâcle, Nana,* and *La Conquête de Plassans*

We have seen that the *Rougon-Macquart* series does not allow the reader to follow the genesis of Napoleon III's political power in great detail. When one first encounters the emperor in *Son Excellence Eugène Rougon* (excluded here are the fleeting glimpses of him that the reader is given in *La Curée*), Napoleon III is already established in a position of authority. But while the series does not portray his rise, it does detail to a greater extent his fall in *La Débâcle*. This is consistent with Marx's analysis of the general equivalent. The sudden disappearance of the transcendence of that equivalent reduces it immediately, catastrophically to a mere element of the system which it previously governed in an uncontested manner. The transcendental aura hides, and when it disappears, it reveals what was hidden—gold as a mere commodity, the ruler as a mere mortal.[1] Whereas the process by which the general equivalent reached its position of transcendence cannot be directly expressed in narrative terms without undermining the very sovereignty of that equivalent by exposing it as merely one among other elements, once the general equivalent loses its sovereign position, it is henceforth a viable subject for narrative discourse.

The disastrous undermining of the general equivalent's transcendence results in what is termed inflation in the economic sphere. It would seem that a comparable political process can be discerned in *La Débâcle*. *La Débâcle* is a novel that treats the outcome of rampant inflation in the political sphere, an inflation leading to a crash, a bankruptcy. The emperor is presented in the text as nothing more than an empty sign of a political authority now utterly without foundation. "Thus the emperor . . . no longer possessed a throne, having turned his powers over to the empress- regent; this chief-of-staff . . . no longer commanded since he had ceded the supreme command to Field Marshal Bazaine" (5:669). The emperor is without the central material object of his office, his throne, and has abdicated one of his fundamental prerogatives, the right to make war. The emptiness of the person of the emperor is emphasized throughout the novel by the motif of spectrality. The very corporeality of Napoleon III is repeatedly denied. "The regiments of the Twelfth Army, in front of whom he was passing, watched him come and then disappear like a specter, without a salute, without a cheer" (5:580). Elsewhere, one of the main characters of the novel, Maurice Levasseur, sees the emperor as nothing more than a shadow projected onto curtains in a window: "As he turned his head, a strange sight plunged him into increasing anguish: the corner window of the notary's house was still lit up, and at regular intervals, the shadow of the emperor was clearly visible outlined in profile against the light" (5:496).[2] As if this were not enough, the emperor's ill health is ever-present in the narrative, gnawing at his physical presence from within: "But he appeared even more tired. . . . An expression of secretly endured suffering made his pale face turn more livid" (5:496). Ultimately, the actual presence of Napoleon III in the theater of operations around Sedan is questioned: "Others were saying that he was no longer there, that he had fled, leaving one of his aides dressed in his uniform, like a puppet whose striking resemblance continued to fool the army" (5:562).

To describe *La Débâcle* as a novel in which runaway inflation leads to a final crash is, I think, to do more than simply use a metaphorical image. The French army, locked in a struggle with the Prussians, is sorely in need of leadership. At the very moment when Napoleon III is called upon to deliver the authority with which his central function as general equivalent has supposedly endowed him, his pockets are empty, his credit destroyed, his worthlessness exposed. An empty sign, he has become as superfluous as a paper note the value of which has undergone a catastrophic devaluation. "This miserable emperor, this poor wretch, who no longer had a place in his own empire, was going to be swept along like a useless and bothersome package, a simple piece of the army's baggage" (5:459). The relation between *La Débâcle* and the novel which directly precedes it, *L'Argent*, is suggestive. *L'Argent* is marked by a fantastic financial crash caused by stock shares whose value becomes totally out of proportion to the material assets they represent. This worthless paper brings Saccard's financial empire crashing down. Saccard's own mask of ostentatious wealth disappears to reveal the emptiness behind it. Of this more shall be said later.

The shadowy spectrality of Napoleon III possesses a negative connotation in *La Débâcle*, since it signifies a lack of mastery precisely when mastery is called for. However, the motif of the shadow is not always or only a negative one. Naomi Schor's analysis of Napoleon III as circulating empty square already suggests a positive quality implied in the description of the emperor as shadow, namely, his function as mediator.[3] In order to pursue this further, let us turn for a moment to a closer study of Zola's descriptive strategy with respect to the physical appearance of Napoleon III. The reader will recall that the baptismal procession in *Son Excellence Eugène Rougon* is of a theatrical nature: large avenues and expansive settings serve as a stage around which spectators gather to catch a glimpse of the principal figures involved in the ceremony. Formal occasions such as this often serve as backdrops for appearances of Napoleon III in the *Rougon-Macquart*. In *Son Excellence* alone, the reader meets him at a reception, during an outing at Compiègne, and during a meeting of his Council of Ministers. There is a repetitive quality about the descriptions of the emperor at these moments. To describe his face, for instance, Zola regularly uses adjectives such as *languid, gloomy, vague, lifeless, impenetrable* (*mou, morne, vague, éteint, impénétrable*).[4] One soon becomes convinced that what is really at stake in this descriptive structure is a *mask*—a theatrical accoutrement attached to the person of Napoleon III.

The adjectives used to compose that mask form a singular constellation. Excluding *impénétrable* for a moment, *mou, morne, vague,* and *éteint* all contain a common semantic feature. One could call this feature something like "absence of distinguishing qualities." All of these adjectives serve to describe things lacking any striking physical characteristics that might cause them to stand out and be readily identifiable. Such descriptive words empty the object of specific qualities, of specificity itself; they carry it into the realm of generality in which it obtains the potentiality to assume any shape, color, or other quality as soon as that quality presents itself. *Impénétrable* functions as a summation of the whole descriptive constellation. If Napoleon III's face is nothing but a source of potentiality, then there is really nothing to seek behind it. It is quite literally "impenetrable," a neutral surface ready to lend itself to whatever possibility a given situation presents.

The mask that Zola carefully constructs is directly related to what has been said of the emperor up to this point. He has been analyzed in terms of a problematic of the simulacrum, in terms of his willful attempt to confuse his life with that of his uncle. The reader has seen that Bonapartism itself works to appear as a republicanism and that with Napoleon III, the very concept of the state as representative of a class or classes is emptied of its content. Bonapartism is simply whatever is politically expedient. In short, Zola provides Napoleon III with a face that is characteristic of his political practice, a face that can change and adapt according to contexts and needs, a face into which each citizen can read what he wants. Zola's description of Napoleon ultimately becomes more than a treatment of this one isolated political figure. The elements he emphasizes are not particular only to Napoleon III; they are instead archetypal traits of any political figure. Precisely because the possessor of political power is one person who must relate to a multiplicity of persons, he must divest himself of his specificity in order to become a common denominator. As Michel Serres writes, "It suffices to keep in mind the star-shaped structure of the one-to-many relationship, and these things, which are already simple, become clear. The whore or the statesman have a relationship only with the multitude. They must become common denominators. . . . The public figure dons the theatrical mask, which the Latins called *persona* . . . pure abstract phantom which each observer believes he recognizes."[5]

Prostitute, politician, actor: all flee particularity and singularity in order to attain the potentiality for change and substitution contained in stereotyped conventionality. Like a passkey that can open any number of locks because its overly specific ridges and patterns have been smoothed over, the political figure attracts clients with his vagueness. In essence, the mask motif allows us to approach the problematic of the general equivalent from another angle. Taken together, the generality, lack of specificity, and potentiality of the mask constructed for the emperor reproduce quite accurately the characteristics of the general equivalent. An element can become the general equivalent in a system only when its origin—that is, its own historical specificity—is no longer evident. In his treatment of Napoleon III as simulacrum, as one who willfully subverts political ideologies, and, finally, as possessor of a mask, Zola touches on certain fundamental aspects of the mechanisms of political representation.

The preceding discussion of the significance of the mask receives strong confirmation toward the end of the *Rougon-Macquart* series in a scene during which Zola reemphasizes the importance of the mask by allowing the reader to witness a moment of unmasking. In *La Débâcle*, as the battle between the Prussians and the French rages outside Sedan at Bazeilles, the emperor suddenly rides onto the battlefield with his staff. Delaherche, one of the characters in the novel who happens to be at the site of the battle, glimpses the group of horsemen and nearly fails to recognize Napoleon: "Wasn't that the emperor with his whole staff? [Delaherche] hesitated, even though he boasted of knowing the emperor personally, since he had nearly spoken to him at Baybel. Then his mouth fell open. It was indeed Napoleon III, who seemed taller on horseback. His mustache was so carefully waxed and his cheeks so red that [Delaherche] immediately judged him to be younger, made up like an actor. Surely he had put on makeup" (5:579). The battle is subsequently lost, and as a result of that defeat, the emperor must forfeit his political power. The defeat and loss of power are clearly delineated by a second glimpse of the emperor given to the reader a few pages later: "Beneath the anguished perspiration of this march toward defeat, the makeup had disappeared from his cheeks, the waxed mustache had gone limp, was hanging down, his ashen face expressed the stunned pain of an agony" (5:621). At precisely the moment in which all is lost, the emperor's mask dissolves to reveal the "man" behind the mask, in other words, to signify the shift from the public to the private sphere. The emperor is left with nothing but his own personal agony. This revelation of personal feelings initiates a process of increasing specificity and signals the loss of generality and potentiality without which one cannot function as a political figure. The unmasking of Napoleon furnishes a counterproof both of the mask's function and of its central importance.

In the context of the mask, the importance of the shadow motif becomes more evident. Its occurrence in *La Débâcle* does not mark the only time the reader encounters it in *Les Rougon-Macquart*. The outing at Compiègne recounted in *Son Excellence Eugène Rougon* furnishes the first occasion for Zola's use of the motif in his description of Napoleon III. A scene unfolds in which Eugène Rougon is shown strolling in the garden outside the emperor's château at Compiègne after an evening meal. He happens to glance at the château's façade, upon which he picks out the emperor's window, still lighted despite the late hour: "And he stopped to observe a brightly lit window on the left side of the façade; lights in the other windows were being extinguished, and soon it alone pierced the sleepy mass of the château with its flaming glow. The emperor was staying up late. Abruptly, [Rougon] thought he saw a shadow, an enormous head skewered by the ends of a mustache" (2:176). Though in Zola's work windows are usually transparent openings through which one sees rather well, the emperor's window produces only a shadow. That shadow, however, is charged with significance: it clearly represents another form of the mask analyzed above. In the shadowy form, the beholder confronts an indefinite and nonspecified figure, one that is totally blank except for the barest of outlines. The degree of nonspecificity is even greater than in the case of the mask.

More interesting still is the fact that the political significance of the shadow described above is suggestively clarified by Rougon's musings as he observes it. Rougon, a political animal in his own right, possesses the necessary acuity to expose the workings of the scene he has observed. On the one hand, it indicates the secret maneuvering of power behind closed doors: "Often [Napoleon III] made decisions at night. It was during the night that he signed decrees, wrote manifestos, removed ministers" (ibid.). The shadowy veil conceals decisions that affect the farthest reaches of public life. It is the seat of a seemingly boundless potential for the exercise of political power. On the other hand, however, the shadow hides the private specificity of the public figure, the parts of him that, if revealed, would undo his public image and end his mastery: "[Rougon] couldn't help but remember an anecdote: the emperor, wearing a blue apron and a policeman's cap made out of a piece of newspaper, hanging cheap wallpaper in a room in the Trianon where he planned to keep one of his mistresses" (ibid.). The blank outline visible to the observer must obscure such penchants and particularities in order to assure the public mastery of the sovereign. Rougon's political apprenticeship is complete with his realization of the double significance of the projected shadow. In fact, Napoleon III is part of a process, a mere element in a system. His arrival in a position of mastery is not solely his own doing; his transcendence is fabricated: "His band of followers put him where he is!" (ibid.).

As we saw above, a similar scene recurs in *La Débâcle* with Maurice Levasseur assuming Rougon's position as observer. There are important differences, however, between Rougon's reactions and those of Maurice. The potential for the exercise of political mastery is no longer a fundamental aspect of Maurice's thoughts as he watches the shadow. One might have expected him to express a sense of reassurance, a relief at the fact that the supreme commander is present and preparing a victorious campaign. Instead, the shadow provokes nothing but increased worry and consternation: "As he turned his head, a strange sight plunged him into increasing anguish . . ." (5:496). In *La Débâcle,* the potentiality that earlier characterized the shadow is undermined by the pervasive feeling of emptiness provoked by the increasing chaos marking the coming disaster. The suspicion of those surrounding Napoleon III is that far from signifying a potentiality, the enigmatic outline of the emperor now points rather to a growing vacuum. When Zola returns to the same perspective two pages later, the emperor's pacing behind the curtain is linked suggestively to the disease that is sapping his energy and rendering him even more helpless: "And upon the thin, bourgeois curtains in the window, [Maurice] saw the shadow of the emperor pass by regularly, the pacing of a sick man whose insomnia kept him awake" (5:498). Like the mask itself, the motif of the shadow undergoes a process of exposure in *La Débâcle.* A sign of potentiality and political power in *Son Excellence,* it subsequently functions as a revelation of the fact that the emperor has abdicated.

Michel Serres's remarks concerning the attempt to eschew specificity in an effort to seek instead a level of increasing generality unite the politician, the actor, and the prostitute into a common class. Zola himself clearly links Napoleon III to the figure of the actor: he is described as being "made up like an actor" and his appearances are always spectacles, as we saw above. But what of the prostitute? As the reader of Zola is certainly aware, one of the best-known and most interesting characters in the *Rougon-Macquart* series is none other than a prostitute, namely, Nana. Moreover, Nana's "coming out" takes place in a theater in which she has finally landed a role destined to reveal her to the general public. Is Serres's argument born out in the construction of the character of Nana? Are there parallels between her and the emperor?

A partial answer to that question is formulated as early as the first scene of *Nana.* As the book's incipit unfolds, Fauchery and his cousin, Hector de La Faloise, are standing in the orchestra of the Théâtre de la Variété awaiting the opening of *La Blonde Vénus.* Drawn by rumors that Nana, the star of the new play, will be the newest Parisian sensation, Fauchery, a drama critic for *Le Figaro,* has come to see for himself. The two men encounter the director of the theater, Bordenave, whereupon Bordenave criticizes Fauchery for not having written a favorable column to advertise the opening of *La Blonde Vénus*. Fauchery replies that he has come to see the play before writing about it, and La Faloise begins complimenting Nana: "I've heard . . . that Nana has a delicious voice." Bordenave scoffs at this idea: " 'Her!' exclaimed the director shrugging his shoulders, 'No voice at all!' " If she cannot sing, continues La Faloise, she must be an excellent actress. "Her!... Incorrigible! She doesn't even know where to put her feet and her hands," responds Bordenave. By now, the reader's curiosity, as well as Fauchery's and La Faloise's, is thoroughly piqued. If Nana can neither sing nor act, then why all the excitement and how can Bordenave avoid a total flop? "If your Nana neither sings nor acts, you'll have a flop, and that's it." At this suggestion, Bordenave, who has seemingly demolished Nana, suddenly changes his tone and vaunts her strongly, albeit enigmatically. She does not need to sing and act. "Nana has something else, by god! Something which replaces all the rest." What is this something? It is obviously sexual attraction, but Bordenave expresses it in a curious manner: "Yes, she'll go far, ah! Damn! Yes she'll go far... What skin, ah, what skin!" (2:1098) The first reference to Nana's physical attributes in the novel directs the reader's attention to her skin, to the surface—not to any inner qualities, depth of feeling, or hidden talent, but to the most exterior layer of her being. The play of light and shadow on that surface will become the focal point of desire on the part of those who behold her. In fact, the culmination of *La Blonde Vénus* is the appearance of Nana on stage nude. "A shiver swept through the hall. Nana was nude. She was tranquilly, audaciously nude, certain of the all-powerful effect of the flesh. . . . No one was laughing anymore, the men's faces, serious, stiffened, with nostrils closed and mouths inflamed and dry" (2:1118).

Napoleon III's shadow invites the beholder to see what he wants to see; Nana's skin invites the desirer to fulfill his (or her) own fantasies. It is a skin characterized by its whiteness, its pure lack of distinguishing marks, and thus its invitation to the imagination of the spectator: "white as meerschaum," "marble flesh," "snow-white thighs." It is unmarked to signal that Nana herself is unmarked: she cannot be fixed or frozen in any particular position as object of any singular, personal desire. The potential that she presents is always open to a new solicitation, a different crystallization—without ever being changed or altered by any particular experience. "And Nana, before an audience in ecstasy, . . . remained victorious with her marble flesh, her sex strong enough to destroy all these people without ever being touched [*entamé*]" (2:1120). The key to this remark is the verb *entamer*, which signifies, among other things, "to cut or penetrate" and which is related to the Latin *tangere,* "to touch." For all the times Nana is touched, she remains nonetheless untouched, "pas entamé[e]," and thus, as she circulates among those who desire her, she maintains an aura of transcendence.

With Nana, we are back to something very close to a general equivalent. Confirmation of this fact assumes a variety of forms in the novel, but one in particular is both familiar and fascinating. In chapter 7 (at the halfway point of the novel), a critical and well-known scene takes place. Muffat reads Fauchery's column in the newspaper, a column which reveals the role of Nana as "la mouche d'or," the golden fly. While he reads, Nana is mesmerized by her own image in the mirror: "Then, completely nude, she lost track, she contemplated herself slowly and deliberately. It was a passion for her own body, a ravishment before the satin texture of her skin and the lines of her waist which kept her riveted, attentively, deeply absorbed in a love for herself" (2:1269). Marx begins his analysis of the genesis of exchange with the simple or accidental form of value in which one commodity becomes a *mirror* for the value of another. He later extrapolates from this observation by commenting that man does not enter the world with a mirror and thus can only recognize himself in the other. But what if one element has attained a position of general equivalence within a system? The general equivalent has no means by which to measure its own value. It can only be compared to itself: its identity can no longer be mirrored in the other. Nana's specular contemplation of her own image is a solipsistic pleasure that cuts her off from the other and marks her separation from the system of desire that she governs. "At that moment, Muffat sighed slowly and quietly. This solitary pleasure exasperated him" (2:1271). Muffat is only too aware that while he has fixed his desire *on* Nana (the surface, the skin), he has not *fixed* Nana. She is a figure of substitution and circulation, and as such, she will always escape him.

My contention is that Nana's skin, brought to the reader's attention by Bordenave at the very outset, is a form comparable to that of the emperor's shadow—both are to be filled in by the beholder. The similarities between the two characters, however, go much further than that. One of the focal points of *Nana,* as we have already begun to see, is the relationship between Muffat and Nana. The tenor of that relationship is established when Muffat visits Nana backstage in a scene in chapter 5 of the novel that reveals much concerning the forces at work in her character. Before this scene, Muffat has already had two opportunities to view her: once as a spectator at the opening of *La Blonde Vénus* and once when he and his father-in-law go to her apartment to solicit a contribution for a charity (a scene that gives rise to many ironic effects). Although she troubles him, he does not really fall prey to her until the visit backstage. Accompanying his father-in-law and an unnamed prince, Muffat has returned to see *La Blonde Vénus* and, at the behest of the prince, acquiesces to a visit to Nana's dressing room during intermission. As they converse with her, the various objects pertaining to her makeup and toilet, the smells, and the general disorder of the dressing room begin to make Muffat dizzy and uncomfortable.

After a round of champagne with the scantily dressed Nana and other actors who have filtered into the dressing room, the three men are left alone with her. She begins applying makeup for the next scene, the one, in fact, during which she appears in the nude. As she applies various creams and powders, Muffat becomes more and more aroused: "He—who had never even seen Countess Muffat put on her garters—was present for the intimate details of a woman dressing, in the midst of the disorder of jars and basins, surrounded by a strong, sweet odor" (2:1213). After preparing her arms, Nana turns her attention to her face, and Muffat's fascination reaches a fever pitch while he stares at her in the mirror. It is, moreover, fully appropriate that he view her in a mirror: we have already seen how Nana's specular relationship with her own image will always effectively exclude the other, be it Muffat or any of his substitutes:

> She had dipped the brush into a jar of black make-up. Then, her nose almost on the mirror, closing her left eye, she applied it delicately to her eyelashes. Behind her, Muffat was looking on. He could see her in the mirror, with her rounded shoulders and her bust hidden in a pink shadow. And, despite his efforts, he could not take his eyes off that face which the closed eye rendered so provocative, marked by dimples, as if swooning from desire. When she closed her right eye and applied the brush, he understood that he belonged to her. (2:1214)

The makeup process concludes when Nana puts the final touch of lipstick upon her lips: "Count Muffat felt still more confused, seduced by the perversion of powders and creams, seized by the unbridled desire of this painted youth, with her mouth too red for the whiteness of her face, her eyes widened, outlined in black, burning as if they were wounded by love" (2:1214–15). Everything in her face is exaggerated, unnatural. Muffat has witnessed her while she applies her stage mask, and precisely at the concluding moment, when the mask is complete, he knows for certain that he cannot escape her.

Like the emperor, Nana wears a mask, a mask which, in this instance, speaks of the potential for love—"as if [her eyes] were wounded by love." The mask invites those who meet her to interpret the suggestion of love, each in his own manner. Almost invariably when Zola comments on Nana as prostitute, he reminds the reader of the relation between makeup and role: "But among the men on the trail of this Venus with her makeup not quite removed, Muffat was the most ardent" (2:1241). Later, when Nana returns to the streets with Satin, Zola describes the two as follows: "In the shadows, their whitened faces, stained with lipstick and eye makeup, took on the disturbing charm of a cheap oriental bazaar in the open air of the street" (2:1312). Nana's working face is a fundamental element in her strategy. The mask creates a mystery that in turn stimulates desire; the mystery is an unknown, a blank to be filled in by the beholder.[6]

The parallels between the figure of Nana and that of Napoleon III can be carried even further. We have already seen how the importance of the mask is reinforced in *La Débâcle* by the moment of unmasking which occurs in the heat of the battle of Sedan. Those familiar with *Nana* will recall that the novel ends with a similar scene of unmasking. At the end of the penultimate chapter, the narrator summarizes Nana's career of destruction and asserts that she has fulfilled Fauchery's description of her as "the golden fly." The final chapter begins with an ellipsis comparable to the one used by Flaubert at the end of *L'Education sentimentale*. Nana disappears; scattered news about her whereabouts filters back to her Parisian friends. Her absence contributes to the formulation of a legend concerning her person: "A legend was created" (2:1471). Abruptly, the narrative picks up again with the news that Nana has returned and that she is at the Grand Hôtel dying of smallpox. Her agony provides the opportunity for the narrator to assemble around the hotel all the figures who have been important in her life. When she finally dies, a long paragraph is devoted to a description of her on her deathbed. The reader is provided with a grotesque and detailed inventory of her features demonstrating how the disease has utterly destroyed her face. I quoted a passage above from the makeup scene at the Théâtre de la Variété in which Muffat could not resist the reflection of Nana in the mirror with her left eye closed. In a striking and gruesome repetition, the narrator presents us with another portrait containing a closed left eye, although this time the eye is closed for different reasons: "One eye, the left, had completely sunk back into the seething purulence" (2:1485). A fearful symmetry if there ever was one. I spare the reader further details. What is important here is the fact that the fall of Nana as a force in Parisian society corresponds precisely with the mutilation of her face. The mask that was one of her main weapons is suddenly transformed into a death mask. Once she loses the generality and potentiality of the general equivalent which must shed its specificity and historical origin, she is powerless and, in fact, mortally wounded. It is certainly not coincidental that

Nana's unmasking occurs in a situation linked explicitly with the coming Franco-Prussian War. As she agonizes, crowds are in the street demanding that the French army march on Berlin. This is yet another parallel between Nana and the emperor: two of the most characteristic figures of the Second Empire are destined to lose their mastery in the context of the same ill-fated historical events.[7]

Nana has been described as a figure of substitution and circulation endowed with a ubiquitous potentiality for crystallizing the desires of others. She is in the sexual domain what the emperor is in the political domain. We saw that Napoleon III was linked thematically in the procession scene to gold as a general equivalent. In a comparable manner, Nana's activities in the novel devoted to her are never far removed from the economic domain. For example, at the height of her popularity in Paris, her house is described by the narrator as a veritable foundry transforming gold into ashes. "In her mansion there was a glow like that of a forge. Her continual desires burned within. The slightest breath from her lips transformed gold into a fine ash which the wind swept away constantly" (2:1432). Whatever the source of riches, they flow into her house to be reduced to a common denominator, gold, and then consumed. Curious economic circuit! In *L'Argent,* Saccard will drain gold away from every possible source, but in order to invest it and create further wealth. His machine will be viewed by the narrator, at least to some extent, as progressive. In *Nana,* we are at the level of alchemy—but an alchemy in reverse. Within the alembic, gold is reduced to nothing.

The success of Nana's project can be measured by the amount of gold she can consume without leaving a trace. The foundry is actually an abyss, "un gouffre." The narrator insists on her position as general equivalent in the system by detailing the variety of fortunes she devours. At stake is not just money in any general sense, but rather money from different and specific sources which she always reduces in a similar gesture to monotonous sameness— it always becomes a mindless tribute to her own whims. First, Nana consumes Steiner's fortune, the origin of which is in a banking firm: "In the midst of the collapse of his banking firm, he stuttered and trembled at the idea of the police. The bankruptcy decree had just been pronounced" (2:1455). After Steiner comes La Faloise, the same La Faloise who accompanied Faucherey to the opening of *La Blonde Vénus:* "His inheritance was in the form of land holdings—fields, forests, farms. He was forced to sell them rapidly, one after the other. With each mouthful, Nana devoured an acre" (2:1455). Finally, Faucherey's turn arrives, and Nana makes short work of his resources: "Nana's triumph was to win him and then to devour the newspaper he had founded with a friend's money. . . . The newspaper kept her in flowers for two months" (2:1456). From every corner of the financial life of the capital, money flows in to be reduced to a common denominator—the desire to please Nana. The whims of a single insatiable appetite make no distinctions when it comes to dissipating fortunes; they all serve the same end.

Moreover, on a more thematic level, Nana's red hair is linked with gold consistently throughout the novel. An example is her public apotheosis at Longchamp, when Vandeuvres enters a filly named Nana in the Grand Prix. The horse is described as follows: "The sunlight lent a golden hue to the chestnut filly, like the blondness of a redhead. She glowed in the light like a new gold coin. . . . 'Look! She has my hair!' exclaimed the delighted Nana" (2:1400). Nana's red hair is what leads Faucherey to dub her "the golden fly" in his column concerning her career. Just as Napoleon III circulates among institutions and parties and brings them together, Faucherey asserts that Nana bridges the gap between the poor and the privileged in Paris—with potentially explosive results: "With her, the decay fermenting in the lower classes rose to the surface and began gnawing away at the aristocracy. She was becoming a force of nature, . . . corrupting and disorganizing Paris" (2:1269).

A third character could clearly be inserted into the series of which Napoleon III and Nana are the principal illustrations, namely, Faujas in *La Conquête de Plassans.* Any detailed argument concerning Faujas would cover ground already suggestively explored by David Baguley.[8] However, a short review of Baguley's thesis and its pertinence to the present argument can provide a means for illustrating how Faujas is related to the two figures studied thus far. Baguley's main assertion is that *La Conquête de Plassans* is a novel in which usurpation in the form of occupation of a space or territory is the fundamental subject matter and in which the primary weapon for accomplishing such usurpation is the look, *le regard*: "Here, . . . to look is already to possess, to subdue. And this law leads to another: to subjugate means as well to escape the enemy's glance, to gain the advantage of seeing without being seen."[9] Consequently, when Faujas and his mother move into Mouret's house, their post on the second floor gives them visual access to everything that transpires around them, whereas Mouret is utterly frustrated in his attempts to see into the priest's affairs. Impenetrability to the gaze of the other is clearly a variation on the structure of the mask/shadow/skin revealed in the characters of Napoleon III and Nana. This is all the more evident in that Faujas is repeatedly described as a shadow or as one preferring to remain in the shadow: "This man [Faujas] lived right next to him [Mouret], and he was unable even to glimpse his shadow" (1:920). Elsewhere, "then the glimmer died out, the priest, stepping into the shadow, was now only a black profile upon the gray ash of the sunset" (1:911). The mask motif is also not far away when the narrator describes Faujas's face as possessing an "ashen [*terreux*] color" (1:905), *terreux* being easily insertable into the series *vague, morne, éteint* which applies to the emperor. When under public scrutiny in Félicité Rougon's salon, Faujas responds with "a hard, mute expression like a stone face" (1:959). It is Faujas's superior, Bishop Rousselot, who finally comments, "It's his face that troubles me, . . . he has a dreadful mask" (1:1138). The priest's face suggests the potential for ruthless struggle against his enemies. Moreover, Faujas's impenetrability is doubled by his muteness: "As the priest was still silent . . ." (1:929), or "The priest gestured again vaguely with his hand, a gesture which was a response for everything and prevented him from having to explain himself more clearly" (1:931).

Who is this mysterious priest who provokes contradictory interpretations? (Some see him as naïve, others as consummate strategist.) Although clues to his identity are scattered at various

41

points throughout the novel so that we, the readers, can be caught up in the mystery with the characters themselves, clear indications are given that he is a Bonapartist agent sent to bring the recalcitrant Plassans citizenry back under the wing of the Empire (they have committed the ultimate faux pas of electing a legitimist in the last legislative elections). To do so, Faujas must appear to be *neutral* in order to avoid provoking any parties and in order to bring them back together in agreement on a candidate who will vote with the majority once he takes his seat in the legislature. Only by remaining impenetrable and mute can he appear to favor no party over the other. The process of gaining the confidence of the two strongest parties, the legitimists and the Bonapartists, is long and arduous. He succeeds when he brings their most prominent members together for informal social gatherings in François Mouret's garden: "We're on neutral ground," says one of the guests (1:1094).[10] *Neutre* is the key word from the beginning of the novel, a word used first by Félicité Rougon to describe her own salon: "My salon is a neutral territory; . . . that's the precise expression" (1:938–39). Because he espouses no cause (publicly, that is), Faujas is able to become a "uniting element" between the two groups (1:1096). Like the emperor or Nana, he transcends the parties in conflict, circulates among them, and appears to embrace the ideologies of each. In one passage, his ability to win to his side all the parties and groups in Plassans is attributed to the fact that his exercise of will has enabled him to become "soft wax" capable of assuming whatever shape is expedient.

These few remarks indicate to what extent the presentation of Faujas conforms to patterns already established. In fact, the repetition of elements is at times truly astounding. The reader will recall the role of Gilquin as described in *Son Excellence Eugène Rougon:* he is the Bonapartist agent who poses as a republican and makes the rounds of Parisian cafés. A comparable figure exists in *La Conquête* in the form of Faujas's brother-in-law, Trouche. Faujas brings Trouche to Plassans to keep the books for a home for orphaned girls. As the election approaches, however, Faujas decides to put Trouche's drinking habits to good use and sends him out to cafés in working-class neighborhoods to disseminate propaganda. In this instance, instead of trying to win over republicans, Trouche radicalizes them to such an extent that they are isolated from the electoral process and are totally without influence upon the outcome. Structural correspondences between diverse presentations of the figures of mastery in the *Rougon-Macquart* reach all the way down into subplots and secondary material. In Zola's empire, every Rougon has his Macquart, every Napoleon his Gilquin, every Faujas his Trouche (and might we not say every Nana her Satin?).

Oppositions: *Germinal*

In the preceding pages, the figure of Napoleon III served as a unifying point around which the problematic of political representation was developed. With the analysis of the general equivalent, however, it became increasingly evident that the structures isolated in the context of the emperor have wider validity: they could be extended not only to a lesser political figure, Faujas, for example, but also, as in the case of Nana, to a realm other than the strictly political. One thing is apparent in the three figures that have been dealt with thus far: they have all thrown in their lot with the Second Empire. In other words, they belong, each in his own way, to the imperial regime. Are the structures analyzed for them of use or interest when it comes to opponents of the regime, to the have-nots? Are we dealing with structures that pertain only to those wielding political power, or do we find similar patterns in the case of those who have no power? The answers to such questions might lead us to discover whether alternative political strategies are either possible or effective. Scattered throughout the *Rougon-Macquart* series are a number of portraits of opponents of the regime: Sylvère in *La Fortune des Rougon,* Florent in *Le Ventre de Paris,* Etienne in *Germinal,* Sigismond Busch in *L'Argent.* In order to formulate a response to the questions raised here, a natural beginning point—because it is the most developed of the novels of "opposition" in the series—is *Germinal.* Zola himself invited scrutiny of the political mechanisms outlined in *Germinal* by describing it as a "roman socialiste." Certain recent Marxist critics—Paule Lejeune and André Vial, for example—take umbrage at Zola's supposed socialism.[11] The point, however, is not to become bogged down in a debate about good/bad, or proper/improper socialism, but rather to study the structures of political representation that occur in the novel and to gauge their relations to patterns we have previously encountered. In order to do so, I shall focus on one of the key moments in the text.

At roughly the halfway point in *Germinal,* a very significant scene occurs, namely, the well-known scene in which the striking Montsou coal miners meet with the director of their mine, Hennebeau. Symmetrical construction of this type, in which critical moments divide a particular novel into two, three, or four distinct sections, is not uncommon in Zola's writing; I would cite *Au Bonheur des Dames,* for example, in which three increasingly lavish sales punctuate the narrative development of the novel and split it into three nearly equal parts, or *Nana,* in which, as we have seen, an important moment of recognition divides the novel in two. Such construction is undoubtedly related to the serial form in which Zola's novels appeared, with the accompanying necessity on the author's part of leading his readers toward the next suggested and promised point of tension in order to maintain their interest. In the case of *Germinal,* nearly half the novel is devoted to events leading up to the first confrontation between the miners and Hennebeau. The remaining half of the work describes the outcome of the struggle begun during the confrontation scene.

A brief outline of the scene would be helpful so that we may bear in mind its salient points. A representative delegation of the striking miners comes to Hennebeau's house one evening to request that the company restructure the wage scale, a scale that has effectively lowered wages below the subsistence level and provoked the strike in question. They are shown into the house, Hennebeau appears, and a confused discussion ensues during which Hennebeau attempts to play the miners off against each other in order to defuse the situation. Etienne Lantier finally emerges as effective spokesman of the group and threatens Hennebeau with the wrath of the International and the widespread revolutionary movement it champions. The meeting ends unsatisfactorily when Hennebeau concludes by saying that he will take the miners' demands under advisement, transmit them to the company, and inform the miners of any response he receives.

The confrontation between the miners and Hennebeau is rich in detail and offers many possible avenues for analysis. The contrasts between the two parties, for example, are carefully constructed, calculated to mark the rift between them. Sandy Petrey has written a perceptive article, part of which treats those contrasts in semiotic terms and demonstrates how they contribute to the ideological structure implied by the scene.[12] The polarities are constructed along a series of semantic axes: (1) clothes—Hennebeau is well-dressed, while the miners are dirty; (2) *savoir-vivre*—Hennebeau is at ease, seated, while the miners are nervous and remain standing; (3) property—Hennebeau possesses a beautiful house, while the miners live in hovels; and (4) food—the chapter preceding the confrontation describes the elegant meal that Hennebeau is eating when interrupted by the miners, while, on the other hand, the miners are beginning to feel the effects of the strike through the diminished quantity of food available on their tables. Petrey argues that the confrontation scene, although it ostensibly fails because the demands of the miners are not met, introduces an unsettling element that threatens to upset these polarities. This is what might be termed the "cautiously optimistic" interpretation of *Germinal,* which Petrey shares to some extent with Henri Mitterand.[13] In other words, although the miners' political consciousness may not yet be fully developed, there are signs that the process of awakening has begun.

One of the first things the reader remarks at the beginning of the meeting sketched above is the numerical disparity between the two sides involved. "There was a silence. M. Hennebeau, who had pushed his chair in front of the fireplace, counted them attentively, tried to remember their faces" (3:1319). Quite aside from the fact that to recognize individual miners is to mark them for later repression, Hennebeau's first reaction is to count. And well he might, for there are twenty or so miners, while he is alone. This configuration is fundamental: the one against the many. Michel Serres has described it in *Le Parasite* in the course of a wide-ranging study dealing with certain general and recurring patterns of human behavior. In his words: "The oppressor is rare; the slave is ordinary—in droves. The relation between a master and his slaves is always a relation between one and many."[14] Hennebeau is clearly in a dangerous and potentially volatile situation, one in which he might be overwhelmed at any moment. The potential threat that the numerical superiority of the miners presents is thematized in Zola's description by frequent references to the noise created by the miners' voices. The implication is that it would not take much for them to drown out Hennebeau's voice completely and to turn the confrontation rather rapidly into something other than a discussion. Following Maheu's opening remarks, for instance, everyone begins speaking at once, and Hennebeau replies, "If everyone speaks at once, . . . we shall never be able to hear each other" (3:1321). Precisely! The moment Hennebeau allows the miners to view the meeting as anything other than a sedate discussion, he might well be threatened with actual physical danger.

This could happen, does happen at times, and, in fact, *almost* happens later on in *Germinal* when the miners' wives storm across the countryside and arrive in front of Hennebeau's house. In general, however, and in the present case, the numerically superior group in a confrontation responds, not by overwhelming the person in the position of power whom they are facing, but rather by delegating their power to a representative, to a hero who then represents the angry crowd. "In general," Serres remarks, "the large number *delegates*. Among the slaves, amidst the increasingly confusing din, one or several individuals appear who represent, as the saying goes, the angry crowd or the struggling class" (*Parasite,* p. 59). A good portion of the scene in Hennebeau's house concerns the manner in which that delegate is ultimately designated and steps forward. As the scene begins, Hennebeau fully expects Etienne to represent the miners: "He was expecting to hear the young man speak, and he was . . . surprised to see Maheu step forward" (3:1319). Maheu speaks because the preceding evening, Etienne had asked him to present the miners' grievances. Maheu would seem to be the perfect choice as spokesman for the group. He is really the archetypal miner, whose family has been in Montsou for over a hundred years. But that is precisely the point—he is too much a miner, too much a part of the group to step forward and separate himself from the others—and his remarks do not succeed in silencing the other miners: "A confused discussion followed" (3:1321). When his intervention fails to bring a clear delineation to the discussion, Hennebeau casts about for another interlocutor—first Pierron, "who slipped behind the others, stuttering," then Levaque, "confusing matters, affirming facts about which he knew nothing" (ibid.). In short, the noise level rises again and threatens to break up the discussion in a drastic manner. All the while, Hennebeau senses that there is someone behind Maheu, namely, Etienne, the real adversary whom he must provoke into speaking if the confrontation is to be fully defined. By accusing the miners of being puppets of the International and thus casting aspersions on that organization, Hennebeau finally succeeds in drawing Etienne into the discussion: "At that point, Etienne interrupted. . . . From that moment on, the struggle continued between M. Hennebeau and him, as if the other miners were no longer even there" (3:1322).

There is a sharp contrast between the moment when Etienne begins to speak and the earlier moments when Maheu and then Levaque spoke. This time everyone in the group falls silent; the confused, noisy atmosphere suddenly becomes hushed, and when Etienne finishes, there is utter silence for several seconds: "These words, so moderate on the surface, were spoken quietly, with such conviction and ominous resonances that a great hush fell over the room" (3:1323). The confrontation is no longer in the same form as it was when it began, namely, one against many. Instead, the situation has been transformed into a one-to-one contest between the oppressor and the hero of the oppressed. Clearly, Hennebeau is a good deal more comfortable with such a structure, and it is evident that he was seeking all along to bring it about. By prodding Etienne into speaking, Hennebeau has actually silenced the miners and ended a phase of the crisis during which he was clearly the weaker party. Thus, I would maintain that it is misleading to focus on the eloquent threat with which Etienne finishes his remarks and to consider that its enormity leaves everyone in awestruck silence: " 'Oh, yes,' said the young man, 'we thoroughly understand that there is no possible improvement for our situation as long as things keep going along as they are now. In fact, that's why one day or another the workers will fix it so that things change' " (ibid.). What Maheu originally said and what Etienne now states may indeed have given expression to forces which threaten to undermine the existing system of social relations, and thus one might well argue that the silence is charged with a powerful potential for destruction. However, there is also a negative side to the silence described here: when the hero steps forward, the oppressed whom he represents fall silent—in other words, the overwhelming force which they possess as a group is rendered inoperable. The master has created a relational structure in which he will be able, very precisely, to master the hero, without worrying about the others accompanying him—"As if the other miners were no longer even there," reads the text.

A relational structure in the form of a one-to-one contest is a source of strength for the oppressor. How is this so? On a first level, one may observe that it is easier to handle one person than two, three, twenty; the odds are simply better. However, more is at stake here than this obvious remark. The confrontation begins with one against many, Hennebeau against the miners. When Etienne steps forward as single representative of the group of miners, he assumes a relation with the remaining miners that is formally exactly like Hennebeau's: he is the single representative of the many, one set off from the many. In a definite sense, the single representative of the oppressed group occupies a position with respect to his own group that is structurally indistinguishable from that of the original oppressor or master. Only then does the master recognize the representative as a privileged interlocutor and accept him as adversary. Michel Serres's comments concerning this type of confrontation are again enlightening here: "At that point, the relation between them is no longer one-to-many, but instead one-to-one, the form assumed by individual combats, tournaments, jousts. The master and the slave square off; they have equal chances of winning, or at least, the outcome is in doubt" (*Parasite,* pp. 59–60). As long as the relation between Hennebeau and the miners was of the type that has been described as one against many, the outcome was never in doubt: Hennebeau was in a losing position. Because the confrontation is transformed into a contest between single competitors, the outcome now becomes uncertain. The oppressed party could shortly become the oppressor of the original oppressor, or, just as conceivably, the original oppressor could triumph. The hero is, and the French term is most suggestive here, a *contre-maître,* a "counter-master," "another master against the master [un autre maître contre le maître]" (*Parasite,* p. 60). One cannot simply say that he is opposed to the oppressor: *he is at the same time very close to him, almost like him.*[15]

These remarks need to be pursued a little further. The miners originally came to Hennebeau's house to challenge the mastery of the mining company that allows it to impose substandard living conditions on the workers. Yet in the end, they succeed only in reinserting themselves into the logic of mastery that prevailed prior to their conciliatory gesture. Instead of progressing, they have reestablished the previously existing status quo. By designating one among their number to speak for them, they have endowed that representative with a structural position in relation to them that is precisely homologous to the structural position of the master against whom they are supposedly struggling.[16] When that move takes place, the miners have nothing more to say; Etienne and Hennebeau confront one another alone. Once drawn into the process of political representation, can the miners possibly escape its consequences? It is to Etienne's credit that at certain moments he envisages such a possibility. "Already he could picture a scene of simple grandeur, his refusal to assume power, all authority placed in the hands of the people as soon as he would be the master" (3:1335). The very construction of the sentence, however, ending with the emphasis on the remark "as soon as he would be the master," suggests the real objective of Etienne's actions and the impossibly utopian nature of his intention to give back what he might have gained. To break the circle and abandon what he has acquired would undoubtedly be as difficult for Etienne as it is for Hennebeau, who himself dreams periodically of a simpler life, while never seriously considering the possibility of abandoning his present situation.

The study of the representational structure underlying the confrontation between the miners and Hennebeau up to this point is not yet complete; a further complexity must now be considered. Hennebeau has been portrayed as the oppressor, the master, the single figure occupying the position of power against which the insurgence of the miners is directed. This assumption, however, is problematic. In fact, by entering into the representational configuration of confrontation, the miners allow Hennebeau to deploy his ultimate strategy, which consists simply in revealing that he is not the final source of power toward which the miners' struggle is directed. In the end, the last ruse of he who actually occupies the position of mastery is precisely not to reveal himself, not to put himself in a situation in which he would have to confront the myriad he controls in a struggle the outcome of which is in any sense doubtful. As a rule, the master instead sends out emissaries, lieutenants, "des tenant-lieu." If the emissary wins, the master wins. But if the emissary loses, the master hasn't lost: he was never really there at all (Serres, *Parasite,* p. 58). Thus, when Etienne steps forward to confront Hennebeau, the feeling that the real battle has been engaged is an illusion that is quickly shattered. Following Etienne's intervention, Hennebeau rises to dismiss the miners without a word. Etienne deduces from the director's silence that he has refused the workers' propositions and will not act to end the strike. To this Hennebeau replies: "But, my good fellow, . . . I am not rejecting anything! . . . I'm just a salaried employee like you; I don't have any more say here than the lowest of your pit-boys. I receive orders, and my unique role is to make sure they are properly executed. . . . Bring me your demands, and I'll transmit them to the company" (3:1324).

The whole structure of political representation creates a space for play in which incessant substitutions become possible. There is always someone behind, removed from the scene, to whom one may defer. Once Hennebeau has given his response, referred the miners to someone else, the narrator's description of him suddenly changes: "He spoke with the courteous demeanor of a high official, with the polite curtness of a simple instrument of authority, spurning all passion in the questions discussed" (ibid.). Hennebeau is no longer the director; he is a mere instrument of someone else, a *fonctionnaire,* a civil servant. The Company ("La Régie") itself, for which Hennebeau works, is an organization uniquely suited to this play of substitutions. State-owned and operated, with civil servants tending capital that is not even their own, it is truly a corporation (*société anonyme*).[17] Ultimate responsibility, an ultimate source for the financial and political power it wields, cannot easily be located. The unknown god, "crouched deep in his tabernacle," as the narrator describes it, is always one step further on, one more substitution in the chain.

The two representatives who engage in a struggle in Hennebeau's parlor, Etienne and Hennebeau, are identifiable persons, with patronymics, with names that link them to genealogies. Etienne, of course, has a place in the genealogy that encompasses *Les Rougon-Macquart*: he is part of the family that is the subject of the series. Hennebeau's great concern in the novel is precisely the threat posed to the continuity of his family by Négrel's affair with Mme Hennebeau. And, as mentioned previously, the third major actor in the scene, Maheu, has a family which reaches back to the origin, back to the beginning of mining operations at Montsou. La Régie, on the contrary, is anonymous, nameless. Sometimes referred to as "la compagnie," sometimes as "la régie," its name is not proper but, rather, common. It is composed of numerous shareholders who clip coupons, as do M. and Mme Grégoire, completely oblivious to its functioning, related only in the vaguest way to the acts it accomplishes. Its dispersion renders attempts to deal with it as an identifiable entity extremely problematic. The characteristic dispersion of the *régie* ultimately provokes an inversion of roles in the scene treated here. The miners begin as a numerically superior group and move toward individualization in the form of a hero who represents them, while the company first represents itself through an individual, Hennebeau, who then points in the direction of the anonymous *régie*. What is the *régie* if not a crowd, a mass of stockholders, numerically overwhelming in its own right? It is as if the oppressor not only negated the numerical superiority of the oppressed by creating a one-to-one confrontation, but then proceeded to transform himself into the very myriad that was at first the privileged form of the oppressed.

It is now appropriate to step back and view at another level the representational process at stake in the confrontation between Hennebeau and the miners. There are essentially two stages in the evolution of this process as described in the scene: the period of confusion during which everyone speaks at the same time, followed by the moment when Etienne asserts himself and addresses Hennebeau. It would be instructive to broaden the temporal field upon which we have been concentrating in order to encompass the periods just before and just after the scene in question and to push the analysis a little further. All the miners of Montsou do not come to Hennebeau's house—only a delegation of twenty. During the evening preceding the episode in Hennebeau's parlor, the miners meet in order to choose a representative group of delegates to present their grievances. In short, there is a third stage in the process (chronologically and structurally the first stage) during which there is no defined representational structure, during which, in a sense, every miner equals every other miner, during which the strike is a movement *en masse*. The designation of a representative group charged with expressing the grievances of all the miners puts an end to this original stage. It can also easily be argued that there is a definable fourth stage in the representational process. Following the scene in Hennebeau's house, Etienne's actions during that fateful evening become known to the other miners in the village, and he is consecrated as the undisputed leader of the movement. His position is transformed, one might say, from a *de facto* position into a *de jure* one. There is ample textual confirmation of this point. In the chapter following the confrontation, for instance, the narrator states: "Henceforth, Etienne was the undisputed leader. During evening conversations, he uttered oracles" (3:1328). One does not deliver oracles lightly; one does not deliver them at all, in fact, unless one has been recognized as someone apart, someone possessing a very special status. The process we have been analyzing, then, is a quite well-defined evolution. From the moment when every miner was identical to every other, the development proceeds to a first point of separation, at which time a small group of miners emerge from the mass. However, there are conflicting points of view and rivalry within that group. Those conflicts cease (temporarily, of course) only with the emergence of a single figure who is then identified as leader not only by the miners who accompanied him to Hennebeau's house, but by the remaining strikers as well.

The development of political representation among the miners in *Germinal* corresponds quite closely to Marx's analysis of the development of money set forth previously. The movement toward a centralizing, mediating figure or element is the fundamental point here. Both processes, economic and political, begin with a situation in which all elements of the system are of equal importance. A transformation occurs which implies a transitional phase during which several elements appear as first among equals. Finally, a single element emerges and fixes the relations that had wavered and been uncertain up to that point. The universal equivalent, as mediator of the whole system of exchange, is an element that is necessarily excluded from the realm of the other elements of which it is a mediator. Gold is no longer a mere commodity; it seems to embody the very value of which it is the sign. In short, it becomes an abstraction, a *transcendental* concept given from outside the system of commodities it governs. Etienne's position in the context of the miners is one of universal equivalence once he becomes the recognized leader of the strike movement. Where the text reads, "During evening conversations, he uttered oracles," the term *oracle* does not appear by accident. It alludes clearly to the transcendental aura of the one who is set apart as mediator. The organization of the strike as well as the work of interpreting its significance now pass through Etienne. With the independent and powerful position he occupies, it is not surprising that his origins as simple worker are temporarily forgotten by others and by himself as well. On the contrary, it is within the logic of the structure developed that he should become ambitious, begin to dream grandiose dreams, and finally lose his original simple desire to help his fellow miners.

Admittedly, Zola's description of Etienne is none too glowing. The would-be revolutionary often has the unpleasant air of a social climber, a careerist: "He was climbing up a notch, he was becoming a part of the hated bourgeoisie, with a certain spiritual and material satisfaction which he would not acknowledge to himself"

(3:1328). Numerous other similar passages could be cited. The struggle for power among the miners appears invariably to create militants who then work for personal aggrandizement. Zola's description of Etienne is no more biting than his descriptions of others who share the limelight of leadership at various moments—Rasseneur, for example. Pluchart himself, the International's provincial representative, does not escape Zola's at times critical eye: "For five years now, he had not even handled a grinder, and he took care of his appearance, combed his hair neatly, proud of his success as a speaker" (3:1344). One cannot disagree with a Marxist critic such as Paule Lejeune, who accuses Zola of mouthing the bourgeois ideology concerning the working class. There are always many ways in which one cannot transcend one's historical context. And yet when Etienne is sidetracked into a quest for personal glory, the failure involved is more fundamental; the problem is not simply one of the author's private point of view or social origin. Once Etienne assumes the position of representative of the oppressed miners, he necessarily assumes a position of mastery that is structurally indistinguishable from the position of the master against whom he is struggling; the logic is inescapable. Whether or not it is possible to engage in an altogether different kind of confrontation, to avoid the situation of mastery described here—in short, to portray a "good" militant, one who does not betray his charge—is much more problematic than it might at first appear. The process of symbolicity, described by Marx in the genesis of money and repeated in *Germinal* when the miners choose a leader, has the inconvenience in the strikers' case of diverting and ultimately negating their numerical superiority.

Etienne does not remain undisputed leader for long. In fact, *Germinal* is justly famous for a passage in which the whole process of representation which we have been analyzing is temporarily overthrown and abandoned, namely, in the riot scenes during which the miners storm and destroy Jean-Bart and Crèvecoeur and finally return to Montsou, where the women murder and castrate Maigrat. Henri Mitterand has constructed an interesting hypothesis concerning the riot in *Germinal,* as well as the two other murders committed by the miners—that of the soldier by Jeanlin and that of Cécile by Bonnemort. In each case, the victim is in a clear sense attached to the power against which the miners are struggling. By the grace of the company, Maigrat owns a store monopolizing to such an extent the sale of provisions in the mining town that he is free to exploit the miners—usually by exchanging food for sexual favors from the wives and daughters of the miners. The soldier killed by Jeanlin is a member of the force sent by the regional government to protect the mine during the strike. Finally, Cécile is the daughter of M. and Mme Grégoire, who own part of the Montsou mine and live from the dividends they collect by virtue of their ownership. But although Maigrat, the soldier, and Cécile are indeed linked to the source of power against which the miners are fighting, they are fundamentally secondary, of no effective significance in the struggle. Writes Mitterand, "Everything seems organized such that for each practical action taken by the working class in order to attack the real power of the bourgeoisie, a sacrificial rite is substituted, presided over, furthermore, by marginal acolytes (women, children, old people)."[18] Not only are the victims secondary, but those who kill them also—Bonnemort, Jeanlin, the miners' wives.

This is undoubtedly a very convincing argument. Mitterand maintains that the diversion and ultimate dispersion of the miners' force is the result of the fact that the miners have not yet reached a stage at which revolution would be possible. "The discourse and the acts of their revolt are themselves inhabited by myth. They symbolize, as such, an infantile stage of the working-class movement."[19] My own argument has demonstrated the complexity and perplexities involved in the attempt to confront an oppressor: that attempt always runs the great risk of missing its mark. But perhaps the miners' wives are not quite as off-target as they might at first seem when they vent their anger through the murder and castration of Maigrat. The phallus they display is one of the centralizing symbolic elements or universal equivalents that stands in a relation of homology to gold as Marx analyzes it in the first chapter of *Capital*. As Goux has emphasized in his reading of Freud and Lacan in light of Marx, psychic development goes through stages that correspond quite closely to the genesis of money. [20] The developing psyche formulates a series of equations based on partial instinctual objects (breast, nipple, finger, the corner of a blanket, and so on). Any number of objects can serve this purpose, but none succeeds in imposing itself, in unifying the diverse objects and organizing the system. The phallus ultimately emerges to provide that unity, to end the stage of polymorphous sexuality that characterizes the immature psyche. Moreover, the exclusion of the phallus from the system of which it has become the mediating element is played out in the scenario of castration. Might it not be that the women, in the course of what Mitterand calls their ritual sacrifice, are closer to comprehending the symbolic process of which we have been speaking than it might at first appear? The castration of Maigrat is at the most banal level simple revenge. But the member which is displayed and villified is a general equivalent. To call attention to it and destroy it is, at least symbolically, to come very close to the recognition of the precise political strategy by which the miners are oppressed. In the end, it may well be impossible to recuperate Zola's text for the workers' movement—the women's gesture is of questionable political efficacy. However, it would seem to be the location of a crack, a *béance,* where a viable strategy for the politically oppressed group of miners is awaiting development.[21]

That *béance,* however, is destined to remain an empty potentiality in *Germinal.* The riotous violence of the women ends with no measurable gains, and the strike itself will serve only to weaken the workers, at least for the immediate future. To confront the Régie has ultimately meant to fall victim to the structure of representation which can easily deflect threats of this nature. Other opponents of the regime—Sigismond Busch in *L'Argent,* for example—will learn the same lesson, as we shall see. Sigismond will attempt to recuperate the work of speculators like Aristide Saccard, only to discover that it is his own work which is ultimately recuperated. Whether it be in the political domain, about which I have been speaking, or in the economic domain, to which we shall now move, the empire's organization seems capable of constant adjustment leading toward an increasingly efficient level of integration and functioning.

3. Deeds and Incest: *La Curée*

I n a general sense, the assertion that politics and economics are closely related in *Les Rougon-Macquart* is hardly a revolutionary statement. The reader finds the two inextricably linked, if not almost assimilated, on nearly every page of certain novels in the series. As the focus of the present study now turns more directly toward economic questions, my intention will be to identify precise points of articulation between the two domains, points at which the strategies of Napoleon III find correlations in the economic practices his reign inspires. The economic mechanisms at work in the *Rougon-Macquart* must consequently be studied with as much care as has already been given to political mechanisms. There is no dearth of materials here. In fact, one could argue convincingly that the framework of the whole series hinges as much on three novels treating economic questions as it does on any other novel or group of novels. The three works in question are *La Curée, Au Bonheur des Dames,* and *L'Argent*. They punctuate the series with an uncommon regularity. After the introductory novel, *La Fortune des Rougon,* which establishes the Rougon-Macquart family and inserts it into the politico-military machinations of the Second Empire's foundations, the reader is brought to Paris in *La Curée* and given a description of the financial and economic practices to which the empire gave rise. At the other end of the series, the politico-military fiasco at Sedan in *La Débâcle* is preceded and announced by a crash on the stock exchange in *L'Argent*. Halfway between (the eleventh in the series of twenty novels) is *Au Bonheur des Dames* in which Octave Mouret, who was given up as a lost cause by his father in *La Conquête de Plassans* but reincarnated in *Pot-Bouille*, makes his fortune in a department store catering to women in their frenetic search to follow fashion trends. It appears hardly plausible to treat the near-symmetrical manner in which economic novels appear in the series as mere coincidence. On the contrary, this signals on a structural level the centrality of economic questions within Zola's work.

In his preface to the first of the three economic novels, *La Curée*, Zola outlines his subject in unmistakable terms: "In the natural and social history of a family under the Second Empire, *La Curée* marks the moment of gold and the flesh" (1:1583). The "and" which marks the intermingling of the two topics will assume its most characteristic form in the incestuous relationship between Renée and Maxime—and its repercussions. After a preliminary chapter which plunges the reader into the Saccard household at the height of its glory, the second chapter of *La Curée* traces the history of Aristide Saccard's rise to financial power. One discovers that he arrived in Paris shortly after the coup d'état of 2 December 1851, hoping to share in the fruits of the new regime despite having committed the faux pas of supporting the wrong side during the anti-Bonapartist rebellion in Plassans. Saccard's brother, Eugène Rougon, is able to procure him a position despite his earlier mistake. The year of uncertainty following the military coup finds Saccard employed in the municipal offices of the city government of Paris, awaiting the occasion to make his fortune. That period, during which he bides his time, corresponds to the year between the actual coup d'état and the final proclamation creating the Second Empire in 1852. Only with the proclamation does the empire really begin as a political entity. As we saw earlier, Zola describes the atmosphere surrounding this moment of inception in rather ironic terms: "The tribune as well as the newspapers had fallen silent. Society, saved once again, was congratulating itself, resting, sleeping late now that a strong government was protecting it and relieving it even of the bother of thinking and taking care of its own affairs" (1:367). Political antagonisms have temporarily disappeared in the silence of an aftermath. Energies freed from political involvement are now directed toward the economic domain, a situation appropriately evoked by a remark such as the following: "The haves were bringing out their money, and the have-nots were looking for forgotten treasures in dark corners" (ibid.). Those out to make a fortune are going to have to do it in a specific way, namely, through speculation. The birth of the empire marks a dramatic increase in the importance of this type of economic activity: "Aristide Saccard, from the very beginning, felt the coming of a rising tide of speculation, its wave destined to cover all of Paris" (ibid.). 59

The term *speculation* is rich in meaning, within as well as outside the purely economic context. Before focusing on the properly economic aspects of the concept, I should like to direct the reader's attention to certain other implications it contains. Etymologically, the word *speculation* comes from *speculatus,* past participle of the Latin verb *speculari,* meaning "to spy out" or "to examine." In turn, *speculari* is related to *speculum* ("mirror") and finally to *specere* ("to look"). Speculation pertains to specularity; it is an activity related to reflections and mirrors and, consequently, tied to narcissism and the problem of alterity or the other. The question of narcissism in Freudian theory could well provide us with a first approach to an understanding of the speculative drive organizing *La Curée.* A pertinent starting point here is a recent provocative analysis by Samuel Weber, *The Legend of Freud,* which explores the imbrications of narcissism and speculation.[1] Weber's discussion comes in the context of a study of the Freudian concept of secondary elaboration in dreams. Secondary elaboration is, in Weber's words, "a process of interpretation, essentially unconscious, designed to throw the dreamer off the track by reorganizing and presenting [the dream's] material in a manner that seems to conform to the logical and rational expectations of the waking mind" (*Legend,* p. 10). The desire to make sense out of our impressions is a characteristic of waking thought that causes us to fall prey to the seemingly logical revisions brought about by secondary elaboration and thus to miss the real meaning of the dream. "To read the dream, we must resist the habit of 'making sense' in terms of the given sequence" (*Legend,* p. 11).

Freud's argument further suggests, according to Weber, that the desire to "make sense" possesses a wider field of application than the sole process of revision in dream activity. Freud contends in *Totem and Taboo* that this desire is at the basis of the very first attempts by primitive men to interpret the world in general, an interpretive activity which Freud calls animism. "There is an intellectual function in us which demands unity, connection and intelligibility from any material, whether of perception or thought, that comes within its grasp" (quoted in Weber, *Legend,* p. 12). Unity and intelligibility are always sought by the interpreter even though the price of such an achievement may be falsification: if no connection between phenomena can be perceived, it will quite simply be invented. Animism comes to be seen by Freud not simply as a forerunner of what will later become rational and systematic thinking, but as a paradigm, *a model of all systematic thinking.*

This is a powerful claim on Freud's part and demands a theoretical justification to support its validity. For Freud, that justification comes in the form of the psychological description of narcissism. As Weber contends, the "all-embracing, comprehensive quality of animistic thought points to its psychological correlative: narcissism. . . . The animistic attempt to comprehend the external world in terms of unity and totality corresponds to the newly formed unity within the psyche: the narcissistic ego" (*Legend,* p. 13). In the genetic development of the psyche, there comes a moment when, in a simultaneous manner, (1) the sexual drives coalesce into a unified whole and discover an object and (2) the ego is constituted. The two moments are closely bound together because, as Freud claims in *Totem and Taboo,* the object of the now-unified sexual drives turns out to be the ego itself: the first object of the unified psyche is the narcissistic object *par excellence.* In its interpretation of the external world, the narcissistic ego will henceforth always project onto that world the very same type of unity and comprehensiveness that it has struggled to attain in the process of its own formation and must now maintain within itself. "The intellectual construct we call a 'system' reveals itself to be narcissistic, in its origin no less than in its structure: *speculative,* in the etymological sense, as a mirror image of the ego" (*Legend,* p. 13). To admit that there might be elements in the world which escape and defy the systematicity imposed by the ego would be tantamount to admitting that the unified structure of the ego itself is not quite as perfect as the subject would like to believe, to admitting, in other words, that the ego itself might have gaps or cracks. "In short, speculative, systematic thinking draws its force from the effort of the ego to appropriate an exteriority of which, as Freud will later put it, it is only the 'organized part' " (*Legend,* pp. 13–14). Thus the narcissistic ego must appropriate the exterior world and organize it into a speculative system. It must deny the alien nature of the exterior world, its irreducible alterity.

The preceding remarks are of fundamental pertinence in Aristide Saccard's case, as one of the culminating scenes in chapter 2 of *La Curée* demonstrates. Saccard and Angèle, his first wife, are eating dinner in a restaurant on Montmartre. By this time, Saccard has had the opportunity to discover the plans for the renovations of Paris sanctioned by Napoleon III. Work has already begun as the couple looks out over the city, but Saccard now knows that much more is to be done. This knowledge is the source of his future strength, for it is precisely by means of real estate speculations connected with the renovation that he plans to make his fortune. In a moment of euphoria at the end of his meal, Saccard reveals to Angèle what he knows of the emperor's plans: " 'Look over there, in the direction of Les Halles; they've cut Paris into four pieces...' And with his outstretched hand, open and sharp like a knife, he made a gesture as if to separate the city into four parts" (1:389).

Angèle, mesmerized, experiences a frightening and eerie premonition as she watches her husband and listens to his explanations:

Night was falling. His thin, nervous hand continued cutting through the air. Angèle shuddered

slightly in the presence of this living knife, the iron
fingers of which chopped mercilessly into the indis-
tinct heap of dark roofs. . . . She imagined she was
hearing . . . distant cracking noises, as if her husband's hand had actually created the gashes he was
describing, splitting Paris open from one end to the
other, breaking beams, crushing stone supports,
leaving behind long and gruesome wounds of crumbling walls. (1:389)

The passage continues with Saccard's hand appearing more and
more like a knife "unable to abandon its giant prey."

This scene represents the moment during which Saccard's plans
come together into a systematic synthesis. Having spent months
roaming about the municipal offices in Paris piecing together bits
of information he has gathered here and there, Saccard now steps
back to look at the whole. From his perch atop the vantage point
of Montmartre, the whole city seems to be in his grasp. He suddenly possesses Paris almost physically, touching all of it with the
movements of his hand: he cuts it to pieces, penetrates to the depths
("gashes," "wounds"), and reshapes it in the image he has formed
from what he has learned. This is the final stage in a process of
"taking possession" begun earlier. From this time forward, it is as
if he has appropriated Paris, made it a part of himself. Without
this speculative moment, Saccard's future economic speculations
would be impossible, doomed to failure. As Claude Duchet has
pointed out and as Zola's text makes clear, Saccard's act of taking
possession really begins on the very first night of his arrival in Paris.[2] The narrator's description is eloquent: "The very evening of
his arrival, while Angèle was unpacking the trunks, he felt the
deep need to roam around Paris, to pound the burning pavement
with his coarse, provincial shoes, a pavement from which he was
counting on making millions flow. It was a veritable staking out
of his territory" (1:359).[3] Like an animal which roams over an area
depositing its scent in order to mark its territory, Aristide stakes
his claim to the city. It is for this reason, among others, that Eugène's request during Aristide's first visit to his apartment is the
cruelest possible for Saccard: "Do me a favor and don't tramp about

the streets. Wait quietly in your house for the position I've promised you" (1:361). Eugène interrupts and represses Saccard's drive to make Paris a part of himself, demanding instead that he remain inside, shuttered. The heights of Montmartre represent the triumph and emancipation of Saccard, who, against all odds, has now appropriated the city, brought it into a systematic scheme. I am well aware that at this point in the narrative, Saccard is still an impoverished municipal employee. However, my contention is that the scene on Montmartre marks a definitive transition into a new stage.

Parallel to Saccard's violent and yet surgical carving up of Paris, observed with such trepidation by Angèle, is a second motif which drives the point home. What first strikes the couple as they gaze out over the top of the city is an impression created by the peculiar lighting of the scene:

> At a certain moment, the ray of sunlight which had slipped through between two clouds was so resplendent that the buildings seemed to burst into flames and melt together like a gold ingot in a crucible.
> "Oh, look!" said Saccard with a childlike laugh.
> "Twenty-franc coins raining down on Paris!" (1:388)

Saccard's own desires are now projected narcissistically onto the objects he observes. The layer of gold that the sun appears to deposit on the roofs of the city is quickly transformed into something much closer to Saccard's own interests, namely, gold coins.[4] The startling optical effect is at first confined to one portion of the city—"toward the Madeleine and the Tuileries." It prompts Saccard to reveal what he knows of Napoleon III's plans to Angèle. The monologue quoted above follows this initial vision. Afterwards, as Aristide and Angèle prepare to leave, a final reference is made to the effects of the setting sun: "They remained at the window a few more minutes, entranced by the shimmer of 'twenty-franc' coins which finally engulfed all of Paris" (1:390). It is crucial to note that little by little the whole city comes under the spell induced by the sunlight at dusk. No part is missing; everything is subsumed in Saccard's vision. He has systematically remade Paris in his own image by excluding everything alien, other, and turning the city into the unified object of his own speculative drive. The narcissism of this process in terms of Weber's analysis of Freud is patently obvious. In Saccard's euphoric dream, two kinds of speculation, psychological and economic, are joined together with stunning clarity.

There is a further important aspect to be considered in the context of the scene described above. In his explanation to Angèle, Saccard is in fact miming someone else—Napoleon III himself. Aristide knows what he does concerning the renovation of Paris because he has had access to a secret document: "One day in the prefect's office, Saccard had taken the liberty to consult the famous map of Paris upon which 'an august hand' had traced in red ink the principal thoroughfares of the second network [of streets]. The bloody pen marks slashed through Paris even more deeply than [Saccard's] hand" (1:391). The emperor himself (in accordance, one might add, with the outline of a project first conceived by his uncle, Napoleon I) has made a series of bloody incisions into the city. Why? What is the fascination for this renovation project? The narrator is persuaded that the driving force behind it is twofold, but still relatively simple, as his explanation suggests. At stake is "the interest of the empire in making money dance, in excavating and filling, in huge projects which kept the workers in suspense" (ibid.). Economic appetites will be served while, from a political angle, the working class will be held at bay. The narrator dismisses the "official" explanation, namely, that the project is conceived "to give . . . normal outlets to neighborhoods previously lost behind a maze of narrow streets" (ibid.).

This official explanation is not quite as banal and inoffensive as it seems. It implies a certain attitude toward Paris which is clearly linked to the problematic of narcissistic speculation developed in the preceding pages. For Napoleon III, there is a veritable maze of narrow streets of questionable accessibility among which entire sections of the city lie "lost." The new system of boulevards will cut through to the heart of such hidden pockets and permit a more "normal" pattern of circulation. One could assume that upon completion, the network of streets will allow Parisians to get more easily from one place to another. But on the other side of the coin, the boulevards will allow the emperor with his police and army to penetrate rapidly to any part of the city. What the boulevards do, in other words, is to destroy privacy and secrecy, to open up the entire city to increased surveillance: nothing within will be allowed to remain alien, outside the realm of the emperor's watchful ego. The renovation project is in a definite sense a narcissistic drive elevated to the level of a veritable political project.

In the last chapter of *La Curée,* the narrator shows the reader part of the translation into reality of the series of red ink marks drawn by Napoleon III on the map of Paris. Saccard walks through one of the construction sites, accompanied by a municipal committee charged with evaluating a piece of property belonging to him which the city must buy in order to extend construction of one of the new boulevards. The narrator's description is eloquent:

> The path into which the men turned was hideous. . . . On both sides stretches of walls, split apart by pickaxes, remained standing. Tall, gutted buildings, exposing their pallid entrails, opened onto thin air with their empty stairwells, their gaping rooms hanging out like the broken drawers of some sordid piece of furniture. Nothing could be more lamentable than the wallpaper of those rooms, yellow or blue squares torn off in jagged strips. Six or seven stories above, all the way up to the level of the attics, one could make out small, shabby rooms, narrow holes where someone's whole existence had perhaps been played out. (1:581)

The project which transforms Paris simultaneously exposes to the passerby the very rooms and "holes" in which inconspicuous and mysterious lives have been lived. In a poignant moment of recognition, one of the members of the compensations committee espies a room which he himself rented for five years when he was a young man at the beginning of his career. The demolitions have mercilessly exposed everything down to the hole for the flue which he recalls having installed himself. In fact, the sight of his old room provokes the former worker into the revelation of secrets concerning himself which the others are forced to interrupt: "Please, . . . we're not asking you to reveal any secrets" (1:584). Shortly thereafter, as the group progresses down the muddy street, they encounter a neighborhood of "petites maisons." A doctor who is among them explains that these were hideaways for the debaucheries of eighteenth-century nobles. The renovation activity exposes secrets that reach back even into the private manners of a past century. Nothing remains unscathed or sacred. Balzac's Paris, in which, juxtaposed to busy thoroughfares, there are hidden, unknown streets containing mysteries of which the average Parisian is not even aware, is to be no longer. The relentless swath of destruction will disembowel the city, leaving no one clear of the emperor's watchful eye. Paris is to be organized so that no part can set itself off from the imperial system. Satisfy the financiers and occupy the workers? Yes, the renovation will accomplish those goals. But the ultimate and more fundamental result is to bring the city together into a speculative organization in all the senses of the word—combining finance, a systematically comprehensive unification, and surveillance.[5]

As early as the second chapter of *La Curée,* therefore, the financial speculator, Aristide Saccard, and the central political figure of the empire, Napoleon III, are superimposed upon each other. This is not an isolated phenomenon, as we shall see in the course of our analysis. In order to begin reflecting upon the more specifically economic characteristics of speculation, a brief detour to recall pertinent aspects of the money form is in order. The illusion necessary for the functioning of the money form consists mainly in considering that the metal gold, far from possessing a value as a product containing a certain amount of work (it must, after all be mined), is rather a simple sign of value. In other words, the role of the metal itself is displaced. Instead of being the privileged material incarnation of value, it becomes an abstract sign of value. The end of this process of development, as analyzed by Marx, is the circulation of paper money replacing the actual circulation of

gold: "The fact that the circulation of money itself splits the nominal content of coins away from their real content, dividing their
metallic existence from their functional existence, this fact implies
the latent possibility of replacing metallic money with tokens made
of some other material, i.e. symbols which could perform the
function of coins" (*Capital,* 1:122–23). The genesis of the money
form, therefore, leads in the direction of increasing abstraction.

A comparable process of splitting and abstraction may be discerned in the structure of economic speculation as it is described
within the context of the Second Empire in *La Curée*. In general
terms, financial speculation is defined by *Webster's* as the act of "entering into a business venture involving unusual risks for a chance
of an unusually large gain or profit." However, there is a more
precise technical definition that is of consequence as well. Speculation is the act of "dealing with a view to making a profit from
conjectural fluctuations in the price rather than from earnings of
the ordinary profit of trade." The *OED* also underscores the irreg-
ular nature of speculation with respect to so-called ordinary economic activity by making a distinction between speculation and
"regular trading or investment."[6] Speculation, then, is an operation based solely on price fluctuations irrespective of normal productive circulation. In the first place, to consider a commodity
simply as a price is to strip it of all its material properties, of all
its use value. Nothing about the commodity counts except its relation to money. In the words of Marx, "As *price,* the commodity
relates to money on one side as something existing outside itself,
and secondly, it is *ideally* posited as money itself, since money has
a reality different from it" (*Grundrisse,* p. 190). Marx has demonstrated that this approach to the commodity neglects the origin
of the commodity's value in real human labor. However, it is in
the nature of a market economy to create a space in which this
origin of value is obscured and can be ignored and in which the
very process of exchange itself, although it is not a fundamentally
productive activity, can turn a profit. In such an economy, one is
not directly exchanging one commodity for another which is destined to fulfill one's specific needs immediately. The existence of

money as a medium of exchange allows one to interrupt the exchange process, to separate buying from selling, and thus to profit from fluctuations in price which occur over a period of time.

This intermediate space created by money is precisely that of speculation. "The splitting of exchange into purchase and sale makes it possible for me to buy without selling (stockpiling of commodities) or to sell without buying (accumulation of money). It makes speculation possible. It turns exchange into a special business" (*Grundrisse*, p. 200). In his buying and selling, not only is the speculator not interested in the actual use value of the commodity involved, his final intention is not even the procurement of the commodity itself. On the contrary, the aim of the operation is to start with money and to end with money: money is the sole motor of the speculative process. The medium of exchange is hypostatized and given the importance that originally belonged to the commodity in the arena of exchange. Speculation is thus an operation that reduces the commodity to one quality, its price, and turns it into a sort of monetary signifier. One of the prime characteristics of speculation, therefore, is the fact that it is *a process evolving toward increasing abstraction,* like the development of the money form itself. The speculator must limit or somehow get around his dependence upon the actual material commodity. This process of abstraction finds its parallel in the political realm, as has already been indicated. The sovereign must obscure his origins in order to occupy the position of general equivalent. He does so by shedding all particular, private characteristics and becoming an ever more general figure whose abstract potential can be appropriated by those who encounter him. From the start, then, economic speculation necessitates a strategy elucidated by the figure of the emperor.[7]

The disappearance of the commodity as material reality and its replacement by arbitrary signifiers (numbers, prices) is central to the description of speculation in *La Curée*. As we have seen, the operations treated in the novel are mainly speculations in real estate. Once the emperor's renovation plans become known, they immediately trigger a "formidable speculation on the sale of lots and buildings which lit the fires of personal interests and the flames of outrageous luxury in the four corners of the city" (1:368). These plans provide the necessary ingredient for creating a process of speculation, namely, the possibility of sharp fluctuations in property values. The owners of the buildings and land to be used for the new constructions must be expropriated before construction can go forward. The would-be speculator need only buy a building that he knows is destined to be condemned and destroyed. He must somehow force the government, at the moment of expropriation, to pay him compensation superior to the original price of purchase. The narrator describes Saccard's intentions as follows: "His first plan was to buy some kind of building at a good price, a building he knew beforehand to be slated for expropriation proceedings, and to sell it at a big profit by obtaining a high compensation for it" (1:390).

The speculative artifice consists in creating a difference between the original purchase price of the building or piece of property and the compensation to be received for it later. One might say that the original purchase price is still closely linked to the use value of the building. The speculator, therefore, must remove the building from the "normal" economic circuit and insert it into a speculative circuit by initiating a series of operations in which the building is exchanged on paper. The more he can repeat such paper exchanges, the further he can remove the building from its original use value. With a little luck and a lot of artifice, the paper value supersedes the original purchase value and becomes the basis for judging the worth of the property involved. The evolution from original purchase value toward compensation to be received upon expropriation corresponds precisely to a switching of registers from the normal economic circuit to the speculative circuit. The deed resulting from these operations is a fictive document composed of arbitrary signifiers (the inflated price) that no longer have a basis in the material reality of the building itself. Saccard accomplishes just such an operation in the case of his wife's building located on the Rue de la Pépinière, which he buys originally in secret through an intermediary. This preliminary purchasing maneuver already initiates the process of detaching the building's value from any link with its actual use as it existed initially: "Using the name of an intermediary, without seeming to be connected to the operation in the slightest, he bought from his wife the building located on the Rue de la Pépinière and tripled the sum invested" (1:391). In other words, the price marked on the deed is three times what he actually pays. Thereafter, Saccard engages in the practice of reselling the building *on paper* to nonexistent third parties (parties whose only contribution to the operation is to lend their names—further empty signifiers—and who are aptly called in French *prête-noms*). These sales once again involve fictive deeds, and not a cent actually changes hands (excluding the bribes paid): "Once he owned the building, he was shrewd enough to have it sold twice to straw men, each time increasing the purchase price" (1:392). Clearly, what is at stake in this process is not the actual nature of the building itself, but rather a series of signifiers, prices (the paper value of the building) that purport to stand for a material reality.

But the members of the expropriation committee, the group that ultimately decides on the compensation to be paid to the expropriated owner, are not completely ignorant. Selling operations that evidence a rapid rise in the price named on the deed are apt to arouse suspicions. The speculator, in this instance Saccard, must furnish justification for a rapidly accumulating value. Once again such justifications take the form of paper operations. For instance, Saccard fictively increases the rents in the leases of those who live in the building, while secretly assuring the occupants that they will not have to pay the full amount. Or he installs fictive commercial establishments in the building, thereby further increasing the estimate of the building's worth. Saccard's sister Sidonie offers to store pianos in one of the shops located in the building on the Rue de la Pépinière, and Saccard and his accomplice Larsonneau turn the shop into a formidable business—on paper. "It was on this occasion that Saccard and Larsonneau, caught up in the heat of the game, went a little too far. They invented financial records and falsified accounts in order to support the idea that the sale of pianos involved enormous sums. For several nights, they scribbled together. After this treatment, the worth of the building tripled" (1:393). It is on the strength of such documents—the paper value of the building—that the expropriations committee decides on the proper sum for compensation. If objections are raised, one might be forced to curry the favor of an important member of the committee, but this is a minor problem, since, at least in *La Curée,* the speculators always have allies in the form of fellow speculators within the committee itself.

The real estate at stake in *La Curée,* then, undergoes a transformation whereby it is reduced to a "jeu d'écritures," literally, an accounting game. Deeds, leases, business books, create a web of signifiers pointing toward an absent referent that no longer comes into play. The actual real estate from which the process began sheds its material existence as it becomes caught up in a circle of signifiers. The buildings and land involved in the dealings of *La Curée* approach asymptotically a mode of existence on the level of other paper goods. They are like bonds or stock shares traded back and forth. "It was a ferocious game; people were playing with neighborhoods to be developed just as one plays the stock market" (1:416). As Saccard says at one point, "We juggle with six-story buildings to the applause of all the dupes" (1:387). Naturally, it is not with the actual buildings that one juggles, but with their paper value, their signifiers. At the beginning of his career, Saccard even envisages his first speculative venture in real estate as the equivalent of a stock exchange operation. "If necessary, he would perhaps have decided to attempt the adventure without a penny. He would have bought the building on credit in order simply to cash in on the price differential, just like in the stock market" (1:390–91). It is not actually necessary to possess a piece of property in order to speculate on its price. The prices at the basis of speculation are signifiers capable of creating their own referents. The speculator, then, is he who masters the signifiers, since fortunes are made and lost in the realm of signs.

It would be worthwhile pausing for a moment to consider the relationship between the speculative enterprise as it has been described up to this point and the goals of naturalism as an artistic doctrine illustrated by the *Rougon-Macquart.* If *La Curée* describes an economic structure which willfully subverts the link between signifier and referent, what are we to make of Zola's own documentary bent, his avowed attempt to reproduce the real in his fictional works? Naturalism would seem to represent a bid to stem a rising tide of insignificance, to react against a world in which one can no longer trust signs. It could be seen as a way of trying to make language and the real coincide in a domain marked more and more by the circulation of paper goods of all sorts. The difficulties of such a project are immediately apparent, however, in the descriptive passages of a novel like *Le Ventre de Paris* or in the descriptions of the hothouse, for example, in *La Curée*. In an attempt to saturate the real, language gets carried away, oversteps its bounds, turns away from the endeavor to render the real and toward a distracting proliferation which the writer has great difficulty mastering. Language feeds on language and quickly puts into doubt any project that refuses to acknowledge that fact.[8] Indeed, the relationship between the speculator and the novelist is clearly marked in *La Curée* in the figure of Saccard, as we shall soon have occasion to observe.

Moreover, Saccard's real estate deals reveal further similarities between the process of speculation and the structure of Napoleon III's power analyzed in preceding chapters. It is clear that Napoleon III himself is a master of signs. The analysis devoted to the mask established the fact that the emperor is able to assume ever-changing positions. His strength is drawn from the absence of any fixed attachment to a given political group. Like gold as universal equivalent, he is infinitely interchangeable. In the specific economic form that the empire encourages at its inception—to wit, speculation—we are once again confronted with a praxis built on perpetually substitutable signifiers. As long as the speculator succeeds in forcing the parties involved in his scheme to remain at the level of the signifier, successful operations are possible. But let someone pierce the web of signifiers, expose the fiction of the paper operations, and the speculative scheme collapses. Likewise, as long as Napoleon III successfully utilizes the mask which is an interchangeable signifier in its own right, his political power rests intact. The moment the mask falls, however, that power is immediately dissipated. As early as *La Curée* (the second novel in the *Rougon-Macquart* series) an economic form closely related to the political manipulation of power reigns supreme. Yet *La Curée* marks only a beginning in the development of this form of economic activity in Zola's description of the Second Empire. The reader is informed very early on that speculation is destined to evolve: "The speculative canker was still only in its period of incubation" (1:387). There is a progression through *Au Bonheur des Dames* and *L'Argent* that remains to be analyzed.

For the present, let us return momentarily to the remarks made earlier concerning the etymology of the term *speculation*. We saw that the word is related to *speculum* and *specere*. That fact was used to offer an interpretation of a crucial scene in chapter 2 of *La Curée*. However, one must not neglect such etymological repercussions as are evident in the properly economic domain of speculation. As the reader will recall from the earlier discussion of the general equivalent, the simple process of exchange itself is originally specular. In Marx's first form of value, the simple or accidental form, two commodities placed opposite each other are recognized as somehow the same. It is clear that Marx understands this relation in terms that give it specular characteristics: "The physical body of commodity B becomes a mirror for the value of commodity A" (*Capital,* 1:144). Now, if exchange is already specular from the beginning, speculation itself is doubly specular. For not only is it a process of exchange, but it also begins with money and ends with money in an open-ended series of operations. The starting point is a mirror reflection of the ending point: money returns to money. The difference between the two moments in the process is in no way qualitative; it is merely quantitative. As Michel Serres remarks, "Saccard is a speculator. In the economic context, the word means a relation of reversal and identity: specular circulation." He then continues by establishing an immediate parallel: "Now, in parallel fashion, in [Saccard's] mansion and in his own family, the same blood flows back upon itself. Among the wild plants in the tropical garden where Renée has sucked a bitter fruit, incest between mother and son (the son being at the same time both man and woman) reproduces, at the level of blood relations, the speculative relation that the father has established for gold."[9] Instead of expanding outward toward difference, incest describes a loop that turns back upon itself in a manner clearly homologous to speculation, in which money returns to money. One must also add that this narcissistic rejection of difference and return to the same is exactly what Saccard and Napoleon express in their attempts to make Paris conform to their desires.

Armed with these remarks, one is better prepared to understand the interweaving of the two themes mentioned by Zola in his preface to *La Curée*: "In the natural and social history of a family under the Second Empire, *La Curée* marks the moment of gold and the flesh" (1:1583). The specular relation is the common denominator linking the two domains: gold and the flesh. Moreover, the imbrication of the two is very precisely played out on a narrative level in the sequence of events recounted in *La Curée*.[10] When Saccard agrees to marry Renée to save her from the disgrace of an illegitimate child, he does so in order to receive a substantial dowry. Part of that dowry "consists of vast lots situated in the Charonne district" (1:382). Saccard, who has been supremely composed during the interview with Renée's aunt concerning the dowry, can barely hide his agitation. "When the word 'lot' was pronounced, Saccard shuddered slightly. Beneath his feigned indifference, he was listening with considerable attention. . . . He didn't move, but his taut eyebrows indicated a great interior concentration. The Charonne lots aroused a world of ideas within him" (1:382–83).[11] In fact, the property in the Charonne district of Paris will turn out to be Saccard's most audacious speculation. What is originally worth two hundred thousand francs will later be sold to the expropriation committee for three million francs. The important point at present, however, is that the marriage transaction marks the common beginning of two speculative processes: incest and real estate operations. The potential for an incestuous relationship between Maxime and Renée appears simultaneously with the fundamental ingredient for the future Charonne adventure. Furthermore, it is striking to note that the marriage itself possesses all the markings of a speculative transaction. Renée contributes a dowry composed of money and paper goods in the form of real estate deeds which she exchanges for Saccard's name: signifier for signifier. The origin of the two speculative domains treated in the novel is itself a speculative transaction.

The Charonne adventure subsequently becomes a leitmotiv that spans practically the entirety of *La Curée*. After the initial mention of it (which corresponds to the signature of the marriage contract), there are two subsequent moments of crucial importance in which it resurfaces in the narrative—both times directly linked to developments in the incestuous relationship between Renée and Maxime. The very morning after Maxime and Renée have consummated their relationship, Saccard comes to Renée to inform her that he cannot pay her dressmaker's bill for lack of funds. His goal is to persuade her (without ever mentioning the idea himself, of course) to borrow money using the Charonne property as collateral. Thus mortgaged, the property will later become easy prey for his scheme. He is successful, largely because Renée is far from being level-headed following the previous night's adventure: "Oh, business! . . . I have a terrible headache this morning" (1:469). Almost as if he senses what has transpired between Maxime and Renée, Saccard suddenly experiences a newborn desire for Renée: "He examined her with eyes in which a startled desire was rekindled" (1:469–70). Because of her money problems and her need to borrow, Renée will subsequently be forced to renew her conjugal relationship with Saccard, a fact which increases her guilt and finally drives her into a state of nervous abjection.

The Charonne speculation is completed only near the end of the novel, and it is precisely at the moment of completion that incest and economic speculation are once again inextricably intertwined in the novel's narrative sequence. To carry out the sale of the property, ostensibly to pay off the debts that Renée has accumulated against it but in reality to collect a long-awaited expropriation compensation, Saccard needs only his wife's signature on the act ceding her holdings to him. Inexplicably, she refuses to sign. He at once suspects that she has been advised by a lover and therefore begins spying on her. "Normally, Saccard did not·seek out disagreeable truths; it was solely his financial interests which forced him to open his eyes which he otherwise prudently kept shut" (1:537). Thus a momentary blockage of the Charonne transaction sets into motion the events leading up to the recognition scene in which Saccard discovers the incestuous relationship between Maxime and Renée: the events in one speculative chain, the real estate deal, have direct repercussions on the other speculative chain, incest. The scene takes place in Renée's bedroom during the final masquerade ball at the Saccard mansion. Renée, rendered hysterical by Maxime's attempts to end their relationship, plans to kidnap her stepson. To do so she needs money, and consequently, she hits upon the idea of signing the act of cession that she had previously refused to sign. Shortly thereafter, Saccard appears at the door and interrupts the tryst:

> A terrible hush fell over the room. Slowly Renée un-
> hooked her arms from around Maxime's neck. . . .
> Saccard, crushed by this ultimate blow which finally
> brought out the husband and the father in him, did
> not move forward, livid, burning them from a dis-
> tance with the fire in his eyes. . . . Then . . .
> doubtless to find a weapon, [he] glanced rapidly
> about. And on the corner of the dressing table,
> amidst combs and fingernail brushes, he espied the
> act of cession, whose stamped paper yellowed the
> marble. He looked at the act, looked at the guilty
> parties. Then, bending down, he saw that the act
> was signed. His eyes traveled from the open ink-
> stand to the still-wet pen, abandoned at the base of a
> candelabrum. He stood upright before the signa-
> ture, reflecting. . . .
>   "You have done the right thing to sign, my
> dear. . . ." (1:570–71)

Two denouements, that of the real estate speculation and that of the incestuous relationship, are brought together in this striking recognition scene. The focus of the passage is the *signature,* which possesses a double significance. While it marks the perpetuation of Saccard's real estate scheme, it denotes simultaneously the possibility of perpetuating the incestuous relationship between Renée and Maxime. It legitimizes both activities by means of an exchange of names, of signifiers: the Charonne property reverts from Renée to Aristide, but Renée herself reverts from Aristide to Maxime. Saccard surrenders his possession of Renée to gain certain of her holdings; Renée cedes the property in order to have Maxime. Renée's satisfaction is short-lived, however, since Maxime ultimately leaves the room with Saccard, thereby walking out of Renée's life permanently.

The superimposition of economic speculation and incest in *La Curée* that is worked out in the narrative sequence is representative of one of the major characteristics of Zola's fictional world, namely, the fact that the social domain has become embedded in the economic domain. Saccard's family ties are an extended illustration of this transformation. In place of traditional relations of familial reciprocity, one finds what could only be qualified as business relations. As has already become clear, the act of marriage itself is pictured as nothing more than a sale: "Then [Renée] thought about the wave of the magic wand which had resulted in her marriage, about this widower who had sold himself in order to marry her" (1:334). Saccard himself is far cruder in his description of the reasons for his marriage with Renée: "His name had been bought for two hundred thousand francs because of a foetus which the mother did not even want to see" (1:386). One might expect Renée to rebel against the material motives that serve as the basis for her relationship with Aristide, but this is not at all the case. "Her contempt had vanished; this man seemed so convinced that life was only a business transaction . . . that she could not reproach him for the deal that had led to their marriage" (1:420). She accepts Saccard as a kind of benevolent banker: "Ultimately, she liked him as she would have liked an obliging banker" (ibid.). Renée, Aristide, and later Maxime live under the same roof, not as a family, but rather as a company (in the financial sense). "The idea of the family had been replaced in their case by the idea of a sort of partnership in which the profits were shared equally" (1:426).

The passages in the novel which develop this problematic are too numerous to cite and would take us too far afield.[12] It is interesting to note, however, the momentary reappearance of traditional family relationships at the precise instant when Saccard realizes he has been duped by his wife and son. The reader will recall that the beginning of the recognition scene goes as follows: "A terrible hush fell over the room. . . . Saccard, crushed by this ultimate blow which finally brought out the husband and the father in him, did not move forward." The situation triggers within him the deep instinctual need to protect his familial right as sole possessor of his wife. Provoked in the most profound refuge of traditional family ties, the incest prohibition, his first reaction is to think of murder: "Then . . . doubtless to find a weapon, [he] glanced rapidly about."

But what does Saccard see in his search for a weapon? "On the corner of the dressing table . . . he espied the act of cession, whose stamped paper yellowed the marble." The ultimate defense mechanism (*arme*) by which he shields and defends himself and commits aggression to compensate for the worst possible familial insult is finally an economic weapon par excellence. A reaction that initially promises to assume an expected instinctive guise quickly reverts to another mode—in keeping with the supreme position that economic motives have assumed in the world of *La Curée*. If the core of interpersonal relationships has become so patently economic, the tendency can only be accentuated as one moves outward from the family group. Such is indeed the case, and the narrator of *La Curée* sums up Saccard's general philosophy with a provocative remark: "Saccard was unable to keep a thing or a person in his vicinity for very long without wanting to sell it or him to earn some kind of profit" (1:433).

To speculate, then, is to manipulate signs adroitly. Yet, successful operations demand that one not confine oneself strictly to the economic domain. In *La Curée*, but also in *Au Bonheur des Dames* and *L'Argent*, the speculator is always more than a vulgar banker: he is also poet/author/actor—in other words, one who demonstrates a mastery of signs in a more imaginative sense as well. "In Zola's universe, to be powerful is thus to dominate the symbolic, to be able metaphorically to assimilate oneself to the novelist, to the master of language who is a specialist of signs," notes Philippe Hamon.[13] From the very beginning, Saccard displays talents that far exceed the merely financial. He is a consummate actor. Having created a character during his early days in the Paris municipal offices—that of outgoing, sympathetic, nervous *provençal*—he plays it to the hilt: "The employee, whose envy stiffened him within, had made himself supple and ingratiating. Within several months,

he became a prodigious actor. All of his Southern verve had awak-
ened, and he took his art so far that his comrades at City Hall
considered him to be a good fellow" (1:366). Because he knows
and speaks to everyone, he has the run of the diverse municipal
offices: "That devil of a Provençal! He can't stay in one place, he
can't stand still for a minute" (1:366). His peregrinations serve a
purpose, as we have already seen, giving him access to vital information. Even as his career advances, he does not shed the character
he has assumed but, rather, puts it to further use. His *provençal*
volubility serves to obscure his real financial situation behind a veil
of picturesque details:

> He had a way of detailing his wealth which be-
> numbed his listeners and prevented them from
> seeing very clearly. His *provençal* twang would be-
> come more evident. With short sentences and nerv-
> ous gestures, he would set off fireworks in which
> millions rose up like rockets and which ultimately
> dazzled even the most incredulous people. This tur-
> bulent mimicry of the rich man was an important
> part of the reputation of successful player which he
> had acquired. (1:436)[14]

It would not be an exaggeration to go so far as to suggest that
in the marriage negotiations he conducts with Renée's aunt, Saccard owes his success to his acting ability combined with a subtle
understanding of literary genres. Mme Aubertot has been living a
sordid drama for weeks, attempting to find a suitable party for her
niece in time to rescue Renée's honor. Fearing the worst when she
comes to Aristide's apartment ("she had feared that Mme Sidonie,
with her shabby skirts, would have a brother who was nothing but
a cad" [1:381]), she instead encounters an elegant, apparently dis-
interested, slightly ironic figure, who puts her immediately at ease:
"When the elderly lady spoke of the contract, he made a sign with
his hand as if to say that such things were unimportant to him"
(1:382). "With his provincial glibness, with a soothing voice,"
Saccard assures her that his only goal is to win Renée's father's
respect. In the course of this single interview, he transforms the

sordid drama into an elegant drawing room comedy: "He finished by winning over Aunt Elisabeth, who, under the influence of this clever man, observed with an involuntary joy that the drama she had endured for the last month was turning into a comedy which was nearly gay" (1:383). Any misgivings Mme Aubertot might have had concerning the marriage of Renée evaporate in the cordial atmosphere of a happy ending.

The art of using signifiers to create impressions which obscure the true facts of certain situations is analogous to that of manipulating fictive documents which dissipate the materiality of the real estate at stake in various speculative schemes. In fact, Saccard consciously links the two activities: one never exists in the absence of the other. Among many illustrations of this coupling of the two activities is the Charonne affair. Aristide creates a complicated and seemingly unbelievable story concerning his partner Larsonneau which he hopes will persuade Renée to sign the act of cession. When he summarizes the story for Larsonneau, his fellow swindler finds it utterly lacking in verisimilitude: "And you really think that your wife is going to believe inanities like that?" (1:525). Saccard's response is characteristic: " 'You are naïve, my dear fellow,' he responded. 'The gist of the story has very little importance. The details, the gesture, and the accent are everything. Call Rohan over here, and I'll bet you I can persuade him that it's broad daylight outside' " (1:525). The substance of any situation is purely a secondary matter. What counts is how one tells the story, how one constructs it, the way in which signifiers are joined together and acted out. Saccard's real pleasure is not simply in making money, but rather, in making it in devious and complicated ways by spinning intricate plots that delay successful denouements: "He was not conscious of the incredible number of plot complexities he added to the most ordinary transaction. . . . He reveled in the impudence of falsehood, the accumulation of impossibilities, the unbelievable complication of the plot. . . . Thus, with the greatest ingenuousness, he was transforming the speculation concerning the Charonne property into a financial melodrama" (1:526).

As suggested earlier, the speculator and the novelist are related to each other, and this link is exemplified by the figure of Saccard.

In the context of his musings upon his own practice, we might well read a telling commentary on the naturalist novelistic project. Saccard could not state more clearly the fact that the gist of a story is ultimately of questionable importance. Plots feed on complexities which distract or amuse the reader: this is where Saccard locates the pleasure of the story. Zola himself as novelist was not unaware of such principles and indeed cultivated them. His mastery of the serial novel form attests to this fact. Suspense, unexpected scenes, the ebb and flow of tension: these are the elements which make up the novel as Zola conceives it. "Scientific" reproduction of the real seems very far-removed from such a praxis. Saccard's economic principles—in particular, the flight into the realm of paper goods and signifiers—lead directly to a homologous literary practice. That practice is consciously exercised and analyzed by Saccard himself. It would not be stretching things too far to suggest that Saccard is another of Zola's masks in the *Rougon-Macquart* series—to be added to a genealogy illustrated elsewhere by Sandoz and Pascal Rougon. In the case of Sandoz and Pascal, however, Zola made a conscious effort to create an authorial figure and was thus inevitably led to idealize that figure. Saccard might well be closer to the truth. Dramatist and writer in his own right, he illustrates the mastery of the signifier which is the now-inevitable necessity of the society in which he lives, one which promotes a circulational play of meaning which is there for the taking for the inventive mind.

Ultimately, the competition that pits Larsonneau against Saccard after their early collaboration is one of literary styles as well as one of conflicting financial interests. Saccard is an excitable dreamer who is fond of complex constructions and *coups de théâtre*. The drawing-room-comedy scene he plays out with Renée's aunt is not really representative of his mature style, which is captured more faithfully by the "financial melodrama" of the Charonne affair. It is always difficult to understand precisely what Saccard's real goal is, what he is really after. In a sense, to win is a necessary but not a sufficient condition for his operations. He is drawn into his own text, carried away by his own inventions; his real pleasure lies in the complications. Larsonneau, on the other hand, prefers a different genre: "His method was less dramatic. Each of his operations came to a climactic moment and then ended with the elegance of a drawing-room comedy" (1:525). [15] His style is one of cool elegance focusing carefully on a successful outcome: "On the contrary, he would smile and charm his interlocutor with knowing glances. He used Dusautry as his tailor, took his victim out to lunch at Brébant's, called him 'my good man' while offering him Havana cigars at dessert" (1:468). Whatever airs he may assume, however, Larsonneau never loses sight of the final goal, the money to be made when his project comes to fruition: "[He] would have sued for payment of a debt even if it meant driving the debtor to suicide" (1:468). Saccard, on the contrary, revels in the means more than the end: "He would have owned the lots a long time ago if he had not imagined a whole drama to be played out, but he would have felt less pleasure if he had obtained them easily" (1:526). The imbrication of authorial and speculative talents is impossible to sort out in Saccard's character and prompts the reader to imagine him as a representative of Zola himself. His indomitable spirit will lead him toward an ever more encompassing goal not unrelated to Zola's attempt to embrace the whole of Second Empire society in *Les Rougon-Macquart,* as we shall see in the final chapter of the present study.

The logic of the signifier, illustrated by the circulation of deeds as paper goods and now by Saccard's literary and authorial bent, finds further exemplification in the context of Zola's description of Saccard's wealth. That wealth, one of the apparent subjects of the novel, is in an important sense nonexistent, a mere appearance: it is itself a construct made of signifiers. The narrative allusions to Saccard's lack of real, solid, material wealth are constant and insistent. The more he becomes involved in complicated deals, the less he seems to earn from them. "He was a shareholder in all the companies, . . . but no one ever saw him cashing in on a clear profit, pocketing a large sum in broad daylight" (1:420). Despite the enumeration of all his riches, "in truth, no one could identify in his case a clear, solid capital" (1:436). When Saccard begins to overextend himself, the lack of foundation in his fortune is metaphorically expressed by the notion of the abyss across which he is forced to jump. "All at once during this period of time, companies were crumbling beneath him, newer and deeper holes were forming across which he jumped, because he was unable to fill them" (1:463). Saccard's situation is reminiscent of Napoleon III's dilemma in the political realm as the debacle draws near: at stake once again is the question of the absence of any solid basis or foundation combined with the art of using constantly shifting signifiers to veil that lack and to turn it into an advantage.

How, then, does Saccard remain financially afloat? By creating a façade of wealth that inspires confidence and thus keeps credit sources open. The façade is to a large extent Saccard's equivalent of the emperor's mask. It is an absolutely essential motif in *La Curée,* as is evidenced by its early appearance in the opening chapter of the novel. When Renée Saccard and her stepson Maxime return home from a promenade that has taken them to the Bois de Boulogne, their arrival in front of the Saccard mansion provides the occasion for an extended description of the sumptuous residence. "The two gates, loaded with golden decorations, which opened onto the courtyard, were each flanked by a pair of lanterns in the form of urns. These too were covered with ornamental gold" (1:330). The description of the side of the house facing the street opens on a golden note. Gold, the embodiment of wealth, is immediately present for all to view. The remainder of the façade on the street is more restrained, but the one facing the Parc Monceau is quite another story. Again the description strikes a golden note: "But on the garden side the façade was even more sumptuous. A royal staircase led up to a narrow terrace which ran all along the ground floor. The railing of the terrace, in the style of the fencing of the Monceau park, was even more full of gold than the canopy and the lanterns of the courtyard" (1:331). Through accumulative repetitions in his own style, the narrator reproduces, in his summation, the style of the house itself: "It was a display, a profusion, an oppressive overflow of wealth" (ibid.).[16]

Wealth, therefore, is something that must be seen, something that exists in the eye of the beholder. The beholder, by taking notice of it, establishes the equivalence between the golden façade and the fortune that supposedly underwrites it and thus certifies what is shown on the façade: "On summer evenings, when the oblique sunlight lit up the gold on the railings of the white façade, the strolling passersby in the park would stop and look at the red silk curtains draping the windows of the ground floor" (1:332). Characteristically, it is precisely at the moment when gold shines in its fullest brilliance that all eyes are riveted upon the façade. There is more, however. Not only do the strollers view the façade, but they can also see through to the interior: "Through the glass panes . . . the petit bourgeois families could glimpse corners of furniture, pieces of cloth, portions of ceilings of unbelievable wealth. They were struck with admiration and envy right there in the middle of the alleys of the park" (ibid.).[17] The beholder sees through the windows and glimpses an interior which is itself of a richness calculated to be as striking as the façade.

The interior appears to be a simple extension of the mansion's surface. A more careful reading modifies this first impression, however. The text describes the perceptions of the interior in precise terms: "*corners* of furniture, *pieces* of cloth, *portions* of ceilings" (my emphasis). The brilliance of the reflecting sunlight on the glass of the windows and on the golden decorations of the façade in fact limits the view, defeats attempts to see inside, and leaves an impression formed only of bits and pieces. Far from being a transparent gateway to the interior, the façade instead forces itself upon the beholder, compels him to remain at the exterior, on the surface. The description of the mansion presented to the reader at the very beginning of the novel already contains the lesson on wealth that the remainder of the novel will repeat. A repetition of that lesson is given rather quickly in a slightly different form in chapter 3: "[The Saccards] displayed their wealth on the façade and opened the curtains on days when they scheduled grand meals" (1:437). When the Saccards conduct official functions inside their Parc Monceau mansion, the passerby is expressly invited to direct his gaze past the surface of the mansion toward the interior. What he beholds, however, is once again a *trompe-l'oeil,* another kind of façade. Such official dinners are, in fact, theatrical spectacles carefully designed to impress the beholder. The curtains are fully opened to allow the beholder's gaze to penetrate only on the days of "grand meals" when everyone is clothed in his finest public garb. To see inside at such moments is merely to remain once again at the surface.[18]

The motif of the façade assumes various forms following its introduction in the first chapter of *La Curée*. It is clearly of fundamental importance, for instance, in the development of the personal relationship between Saccard and Renée. Renée will time and again play the role of public symbol of Aristide's wealth, the role of emblem of his sound creditworthiness. He purposefully encourages her profligacy, not only to entrap her, but also to create yet another appearance of fortune. "He wanted her to be well-dressed, loud, making all of Paris turn its head to look at her. This established his reputation, doubled the probable figure of his fortune" (1:420). And he intervenes directly to make certain that Renée fulfills her function as an illustration of his financial position. Characteristic in this context is his purchase of Laure d'Aurigny's diamonds, an act which, from the very beginning of *La Curée,* takes on the air of a prodigious financial operation and which ultimately becomes a veritable leitmotiv of the novel. During the promenade with which the first chapter opens, the reader first hears of this "transaction" when Maxime remarks to Renée: "[Saccard] finds a way to pay Laure's debts and to give diamonds to his wife" (1:321). In the course of the dinner that follows this scene, the guests at the Saccard house cannot keep their eyes off the necklace and aigrette: "All the women were full of praise. . . . Aristide Saccard drew near, . . . his grinning face betrayed a lively satisfaction. And he watched the two real estate developers through the corner of his eye, the two parvenu bricklayers, . . . who were listening to the figures being rattled off—fifteen thousand, fifty thousand francs— with visible respect" (1:337).

Later, when Renée presses Saccard to pay off one of her outstanding debts, he admits that he cannot because of his present tenuous financial position. The jewels reappear at this point as a possible means of liquidating her debts. This simple and seemingly viable solution is not at all in Saccard's interests. In the first place, Renée's indebtedness is a vital element for the success of the Charonne speculation. What Saccard understands and Renée does not is that wealth is not simply a question of ready cash, of converting jewels, for instance, into money. It is instead a complicated process of inspiring confidence in others and thereby creating *credit*—credit understood both as *prestige* and as *money advanced against pledges of its repayment*. Every visible aspect of Saccard's estate must serve to maintain such credit. It is therefore extremely

unwise, if not impossible, to sell off the jewels: " 'I forbid you to do that!' he cried in a worried voice. 'If you are not seen with those jewels tomorrow at the minister's ball, there will be all sorts of gossip concerning my situation' " (1:465). The jewels are a sign of wealth in precisely the same manner as the Saccard mansion's golden façade. Their absence would be immediately noticed—as the effect of their presence makes abundantly clear: "But what created a stir among everyone at the ball was the diamond rivière and aigrette. . . . They were the only topic of conversation the whole evening" (1:475). What is the result of this "coup de théâtre," as the narrator so aptly calls it? Precisely to reopen credit sources that threatened to disappear: "[Saccard] had just consolidated his credit" (ibid.). Fortune, then, is not necessarily linked to immediate solvency: "On some mornings [Saccard] did not even have a thousand francs in his coffers" (1:462).

What is the meaning of Saccard's paradoxical dilemma—fabulously rich and yet at the same time always short of money? Are we to believe that he has simply hidden an insolvent situation behind a dazzling screen of ruse and deception? Certainly, Zola's text supports this viewpoint to some extent. Such a perspective is too simplistic, however: there is more at stake here. If one considers the link between Aristide's apparent lack of real wealth and the developing practice of speculation characteristic of the Second Empire as described by Zola, one can begin to see Saccard's actions as demonstrations that his skill as speculator results from an important principle which he has clearly mastered: wealth is never simply accumulation, but, more essentially, *movement*. This is the second fundamental distinctive trait of the speculative process, the first being the necessity of operating at the level of the signifier, characterized earlier as the tendency toward *abstraction*. In the new and rising economy of which Saccard is a part, acquiring a fortune cannot be viewed as a simple hoarding operation, as an attempt to extract ever-increasing sums of money from circulation. On the contrary, money must always be put back into circulation in order to create more money. As Marx states, "[Money], as *material representative of general wealth,* . . . is realized only by being thrown back into circulation, to disappear in exchange for the singular, particular modes of wealth. It remains in circulation, as medium 87 of circulation; but for the accumulating individual, it is lost, and this disappearance is the only possible way to secure it as wealth" (*Grundrisse,* pp. 233–34).

The fact that Saccard cannot always find even small sums of money necessary at particular moments indicates in part, therefore, that he has understood a fundamental economic axiom: in order to succeed in the speculative context of the empire, one must always keep one's money mobilized, in motion. Deception is undeniably a part of Saccard's business operations. He does overextend himself at critical moments and must hide this fact from the general public. Nevertheless, the supposed void behind the façade is not simply and only the result of ruse and deception, but equally the creation of an intelligent practitioner of the economics of an evolving market system. The wealth that Saccard creates can no longer conform to the traditional concept of material fortune. His discovery of the direct relationship between wealth and constant circulation would ideally preclude the act of accumulating a treasure by removing money from circulation and thus short-circuiting the economic machine he has discovered and in part created himself.

Within the scope of the present study, it is important to note that the second structural trait of speculative activity is once again directly related to a fundamental characteristic of Napoleon III's political strategy. The reader will recall that the important fourth chapter of *Son Excellence Eugène Rougon* contained a scene in which the emperor was momentarily suspended on a bridge between the two banks of the Seine. This emblematic scene illustrated the fact that the emperor was a circulating element joining together various parties without ever becoming permanently attached to a particular one. Any blockage in his constant movement among varying positions would have the effect of crystallizing an opposition and creating a menace to his continued sovereignty. For the emperor, as well as for the speculator, unremitting circulation is a basic necessity.

The movement inherent in the structure of speculation is textually marked in *La Curée* by a series of metaphors of liquidity used by the novelist to render the perpetual motion that Aristide has discovered. For example, one encounters wealth as an ocean and Saccard as a deft swimmer:

> It seemed to him that a sea of twenty-franc coins
> stretched out around him. First a lake, it then be-
> came an ocean, filling the immense horizon with the
> noise of strange waves, a metallic music which tic-
> kled his heart. And he ventured out upon it, a more
> audacious swimmer with each passing day, diving,
> returning to the surface, sometimes on his back, at
> other times on his stomach, crossing this immensity
> in clear and stormy weather, counting on his
> strength and his adroitness to keep him from ever
> sinking. (1:416)

However, the image of the sea seems intrinsically too omni-directional to represent the flux toward which Zola wishes to draw the reader's attention. He quickly abandons it in favor of the image of the river: "This river of gold, with no known source, which seemed to flood out of his office, made the gapers marvel" (1:420). Or again, "He spent an unbelievable amount of money; the flow out of his coffers continued, and the sources of this river of gold had not yet been discovered" (1:436). Adjectives such as *net* and *solide* used to describe the traditional wealth established through accumulation that Saccard lacks are regularly contrasted with the movement of the "river of gold," flux that must always lack stability. Even the success of the gigantic Charonne speculation does not allow Aristide to constitute a stable fortune in the old-fashioned sense. He is condemned to a movement of continual amplification, to an ever-widening extension of the process he has begun. "Saccard, saved from a crisis . . . naïvely repeated that he was still too poor, that he could not stop there" (1:587). This is what one must call the modernity of Saccard's economic stance as revealed by his insistence upon the necessity of circulation that alone can continue to produce wealth. It is perhaps too early to call his position a veritable philosophy. The theoretical formulation will not come until *L'Argent,* even though the praxis is already well established.

In the midst of a description of speculation as money in motion, one must not lose sight of a fundamental paradox in *La Curée,* a paradox reinforcing the contention that the novel treats speculation in an as-yet imperfect form at the beginning of its development during the Second Empire. The contradiction in question can be stated thus: wealth is a function of the movement of money, and yet the object of speculation in *La Curée* is real estate. The French expressions dramatize the point in a more striking fashion. "Real estate" would be translated as *biens immobiliers,* "buildings" as *immeubles.* Saccard's objective is to circulate ever more rapidly precisely that which is inherently considered immobile.[19] The evolution toward abstraction and toward perpetual motion that typifies speculation in its most successful forms encounters almost insurmountable obstacles when it comes to real estate. In certain cases, the material reality of the merchandise at stake (buildings) can and does brutally reassert its priority over the representation in the form of purely paper goods which seemed to have successfully replaced it. The disappearance of that material reality is an ideal goal toward which one might tend, but which is ultimately unattainable. In point of fact, the speculator necessarily finds himself at some point with an unwanted building on his hands.

An illustration of this unavoidable pitfall is provided in *La Curée* by the story of Saccard's association with Mignon and Charrier. The three men obtain rights to develop three sections of the new boulevards projected in Haussmann's plans. Saccard wants to build stores, apartments, and concert halls, among other things, but his two partners balk at the idea. Consequently, the three divide their land equally. "[Mignon and Charrier] continued to sell their lots prudently. [Saccard] continued building" (1:419). An uncharacteristic fascination with the solidity of the building itself temporarily diverts Saccard away from the correct speculative strategy. Instead of buying and selling as rapidly as he normally would, Saccard decides to build. As the novel progresses, it will become evident that this erroneous decision is what institutes a downward slide in his fortune which will lead him into increasing difficulty. He later realizes he has made a mistake "by building on his share of the lots while they prudently sold theirs. While they were making a fortune, he was left with buildings on his hands, which he could often get rid of only at a loss" (1:463–64).

Thus Saccard's exploitation of the economic possibilities open to him is not without ambiguity. He is still too easily tempted by a project that immobilizes too much capital, despite his otherwise energetic manipulation of the power implied by perpetual circulation. However, this is clearly not simply a shortcoming on Aristide's part, but a more fundamental tendency that is always part and parcel of the underlying principles operative in real estate speculation. The real estate speculator necessarily remains fatally handicapped because, by nature, the buying and selling of property concentrates too much capital in one place, raising the risk of crippling losses when momentary blockages develop. The misadventure cited above reminds us that although the goal of the speculator is to deal solely in paper goods, the material referent behind such signifiers can be only *theoretically* and *imperfectly* obscured. In practice, it always tends to reappear—and this is especially true in the case of something as substantial as real estate holdings. The surprising thing is perhaps the extent to which Saccard succeeds. In any case, the evolution of speculation to be studied in *Au Bonheur des Dames* and *L'Argent* will reveal a definite tendency to concentrate activity around a referent more easily manipulated.

There is a second important way in which the development of speculation to its fullest limits is hindered in Saccard's case. In the end, Aristide *overinvests* in the signifiers of wealth. The analysis of the façade conducted earlier emphasized the importance of this mechanism for establishing prestige and, in turn, monetary credit. However, there is a point, ambiguous and perhaps difficult to establish precisely, at which increased investment in the signifiers of wealth begins to bring diminishing returns in terms of prestige and credit. Such a point is reached when Aristide's ambition simply to appear wealthy is no longer viewed as a means, but rather as an end in itself: he decides he wants to be the wealthiest man in Paris. That ambition drives him to immobilize increasingly larger sums of money in order to illustrate his fortune. He thus creates a tenuous situation in which he continually runs the risk of being unable to pay off the smallest debts. Everything is channeled toward prestige, and nothing remains for such trivial matters as the food bills for his household. This process is a vicious circle: the richer the façade he constructs, the more debts he incurs. But the moment he *visibly* defaults on his increasing debts, all eyes will turn from the façade of signifiers to the absence of real substance they conceal, and all credit he may have established will instantaneously vanish. The wisest strategy would consist in controlling expenditures devoted to show and display, but such a path is precluded once Saccard's ambition becomes unlimited, once it veers toward the superlative.

Perhaps the fundamental illustration of this tendency is again the mansion in the Parc Monceau. Aristide goes heavily into debt to finance the construction of the house. Despite the difficulties he later encounters, nothing can persuade him to reduce the colossal expense incurred by the standard of living he adopts once settled in the house. All of that expense represents money that cannot be thrown back into speculative ventures and thus cannot create new wealth. In the end, a large part of the money earned from the Charonne speculation is swallowed up by the debts on the house. "He paid off five hundred thousand francs of the million he owed his decorator and his builder for the Monceau Park mansion" (1:587). Saccard is destined to be squeezed ever harder by the very logic he unleashes. Hence the bankruptcy he will endure offstage, as it were, between *La Curée* and *L'Argent*.

Might it not be possible to see in this process an illustration of the second major trait of the speculator's personality? Earlier Saccard was described as an accomplished author and actor. Now he must be viewed in his role as gambler taken in by the game he plays. Aristide's grandiose schemes ultimately lead him toward a desire to be the wealthiest, the most powerful. The absolute nature of such a goal suggests that there is really no point at which it would be possible for him to stop. No state or status would ever be sufficient to fulfill his urge for movement, for ever more activity, be it even to outstrip all the other Parisian speculators. With respect to both of these fundamental character traits, Frank Norris's creation, Curtis Jadwin of *The Pit,* is remarkably similar to Saccard. Norris will present Jadwin as someone who is a cut above the vulgar businessman, someone who possesses a spark of genius which Norris characterizes as his "sixth sense": "Again that strange sixth sense of his, the inexplicable instinct, that only the born speculator knows, warned him." Later, another reference is made to the same faculty: "In some indefinable way, [he was] warned by that blessed sixth sense that had made him the successful speculator he was."[20] Why inexplicable? Why indefinable? Jadwin's sixth sense is a sign of genius, and genius, in the Romantic ideology, is precisely that indefinable spark of the sublime which sets the poet off from mere mortal. Howard Horwitz, citing passages from Norris's *The Responsibilities of the Novelist,* sets forth the analogy between poet and speculator as Norris perceives it:

> Norris . . . draws an analogy between the financier
> and the great writer: "the genius of the American
> financier," here "Mr. Carnegie," does not differ "in
> kind from the genius of" the writer. Norris ramifies
> this comparison: the financier is to the "mere busi-
> nessman," who simply markets goods, as the poet
> (or Romancer) is to the mere writer. . . . The mere
> businessman and mere writer operate at the level of
> copyist Realism, handling goods and external de-
> tails, exchanging only stated values. The financier is
> the extraordinary type inhabiting the credit econo-
> my of 1900 America, who, like the true poet, "deals
> with elemental forces" of valuation that "stir whole
> nations."[21]

Saccard and Jadwin are both viewed by their respective creators as creative artists in their own right, although Saccard's (and even more so Larsonneau's) preferred genre is a bit less monumental and earth-shaking than Jadwin's. Zola will not call Saccard's concerns "elemental forces" that "stir whole nations." Nevertheless, the transformations effected by Aristide and his cohorts upon the city of Paris not only provoke deep changes in the living habits of scores of Parisians—especially the poor—but they also promote a type of political power and surveillance clearly different in kind from what precedes them.

A further parallel between Jadwin and Saccard is evident in Jad- win's taste for the aspect of risk in his speculative activity and his inability to define a veritable ending point at which he could stop. If Jadwin does have a specific goal in mind, it is once again in the realm of the absolute as it is for Saccard: Jadwin will stop at nothing less than a corner on the wheat market. The excitement of a grandiose scheme ultimately blinds the speculator to the pain and ruin he may cause around him and makes it impossible for him to halt the process in which he has become engaged until, finally, a crash and the ensuing bankruptcy remove his means of action entirely and violently. In fact, the very logic of speculation as an activity that succeeds by manipulating prices would seem to require an ever-widening involvement by the speculator, who must seek an ever-stronger grip on the movement of those very prices. The more encompassing the speculator's scheme, the greater his chances for success, and thus his activity must perpetually grow in scope. As will become clearer in *L'Argent,* once a certain point is reached, the speculator cannot pick up his stakes and leave the table without provoking a collapse from which even he would not be spared. Rare is the individual who can simply pocket his gains and withdraw. In any case, neither Zola nor Norris would grace such a man with the title of true speculator: the dreams of the true speculator must always overrun reality.

The similarities between the French and American debates concerning the dangers of speculation developing in both countries during essentially the same historical period will be the subject of further discussion in the context of an analysis of *L'Argent.* For the moment, however, I should like to study from a slightly different angle the questions raised by Saccard's ever-increasing expenditures devoted to display. The fundamental contention has been that the main ingredient of Aristide's successful economic activities is his rejection of an accumulational strategy in favor of a circulational one. In his case, the fetichism of hoarding appeared to be broken. His increasing investment in the signifiers of wealth, however, has the effect of reintroducing accumulation into a circuit from which it had been banished. In the final judgment, the impulse toward accumulation is still too strong in Saccard's milieu and within Saccard himself. A tendency to serve the hoarding fetichism by overindulging in the signs of wealth (house, carriages, jewels, gold) seems inescapable. The text of *La Curée* emphasizes this penchant in a very striking scene. During the masquerade ball near the end of the novel, M. Hupel de la Noue presents a play he has written on the mythic theme of Echo and Narcissus.[22] The bored guests in the Saccard household are unimpressed until the second tableau.

> The curtain opened; the piano became louder.
> Everyone was utterly dazzled. The spotlight fell on a
> flaming splendor in which the spectators at first saw
> only a blazing mass in which gold ingots and pre-
> cious stones seemed to melt together. . . . On the
> ground, as a result of a daring anachronism on the
> part of M. Hupel de la Noue, there was a landslide
> of twenty-franc coins: gold louis spread out, piled
> up, a profusion of gold louis which rose up toward
> the ceiling. (1:548)

The view of these piles of gold coins sets off a reverie within the spectators that reveals their deepest sentiments concerning gold:

> The daring nature of the twenty-franc coins, this
> shimmer of a modern strongbox which had landed
> in a corner of Greek mythology, enchanted the
> imagination of the ladies and the financiers who
> were there. The words "Look at those coins, all that
> money!" ran through the crowd, along with smiles
> and long shivers of pleasure. Surely, each of the la-
> dies, each of the gentleman, dreamt of having all
> that for him or herself in a vault underground.
> (1:549)

This play within the novel provokes and brings to the surface a desire for the pure accumulation of gold, a desire that is a relic of a past economic age. However, Saccard himself falls prey to this anachronistic impulse, relishing inordinately the display of the precious metal not only on stage, but on the façade of his mansion as well. The moment of visual fascination provided by the stage setting anticipates the pleasure Octave Mouret allows himself in *Au Bonheur des Dames* when he piles his store's daily receipts on his desk to view them before they disappear into circulation.

The early development of speculation as depicted in *La Curée* illustrates the initial form of a type of economic activity destined to mature in two other novels that will be treated subsequently, namely, *Au Bonheur des Dames* and *L'Argent*. Despite the tendency toward a new mobility in the circulation of money, we have seen that there are two sorts of weaknesses evident in *La Curée*. Real estate requires too great a concentration of capital in one object with the accompanying risk of losses. It is a domain in which the material referent behind the paper goods at stake reappears too easily. And secondly, the urge for accumulation is still too strong and risks disrupting the system. Emblematically, it could be said that *La Curée* is the novel in which gold is on the façades of buildings, both because gold is produced by real estate and because it is still the premier sign of wealth as such. But gold's position on the façade alerts one to the constant danger of a disruption in circulation causing the metaphor of liquidity to veer back toward solidity. Ultimately, the reader's encounter with the Saccard mansion in chapter 1 of *La Curée* contains the lesson of the economic structure revealed in the remainder of the novel. The present reading has been, in a sense, a reading of the mansion's façade. As we turn to *Au Bonheur des Dames,* we shall discover that gold has shifted from façades to Octave Mouret's desk, where, except for fleeting moments, its movement is uninterrupted and where the problem of immobility, therefore, will be more successfully addressed.

4. The Play of Fashion: *Au Bonheur des Dames*

The narrator of *Au Bonheur des Dames* wastes no time situating Octave Mouret's economic activities within that sphere in which exchange itself has become a special business, namely, within the domain of speculation: "Mouret threw himself into speculation like a poet" (3:420). His ever-expanding department store once again illustrates a circulational process meant to begin and to end with money, a business originating solely in the movement of money as opposed to the production of commodities. Moreover, for Mouret as for Saccard, speculation involves increasingly grandiose schemes which threaten at every moment to plunge him into an abyss. As the narrator says of the huge sale that takes place in the store during the second chapter of the novel: "It was a very big operation; the store was putting its fortune on the line . . . with such ostentation, with such a need for the colossal, that the very foundations seemed ready to crumble beneath it" (ibid.). The narrator clearly presents the reader with a second incarnation of the financial poet in the person of Octave Mouret.

Whereas Saccard in *La Curée* was almost instinctively borne along by the tide of speculation and was consequently not always fully aware of the rules governing his own economic activity, Mouret is a full-blown theoretician of the genre. Much of what often remains implicit in the functioning of the speculative process in *La Curée* becomes explicit in *Au Bonheur* and finds clear exposition in the words of Mouret himself. Octave never tires of explaining the process at work in his great store, and his words have a familiar ring in light of the preceding analysis of *La Curée*. A key passage for any understanding of the economic principles applied by Mouret in his store can be found in the discussion he has with Baron Hart- mann in Mme Desforges's apartment in chapter 3 of *Au Bonheur*. Obsessed by the idea of expanding his business, Mouret has discovered that Hartmann's bank, the Crédit Immobilier, has purchased the buildings adjacent to Au Bonheur, the very real estate absolutely necessary for his projected expansion scheme. He therefore arranges a meeting with the baron in order to attempt to persuade him to give up the space to Au Bonheur. His success depends, of course, on his ability to convince the baron that the financial gains of such an operation will exceed what the bank expects to earn within the framework of its own projects for development of the property. The situation furnishes a perfect occasion for Mouret to explain the economics of his business. Simply put, the store functions as follows:

> This type of business was now based on the continual and rapid renewal of the capital involved— which had to be transformed into merchandise as many times as possible during the same year. Thus, in the past year, his capital, representing only five hundred thousand francs, had turned over four times and had in this way produced two million francs in sales. A miserable beginning, moreover, which would soon be multiplied by ten because [Mouret] was certain in a later stage to be able to attain a turnover equal to fifteen or twenty times the capital in certain departments. (3:458)

The main characteristics of speculation outlined in *La Curée* reappear clearly in this passage. It requires not only the constant movement of capital, but a search for an increasingly rapid movement. The turnover in the form of money–commodity–money creates a profit that can be augmented only by allowing an ever quicker repetition of the same cycle. Thus a relatively small amount of capital is capable of producing large profits, but only if one is willing to throw capital and profits constantly back into circulation. There is evidently no room for classic accumulation in this scheme. The danger involved in such a system is evident, for if the

98

near-totality of capital assets is unremittingly converted into commodities to be sold, no reserve remains upon which to fall back in case of failure. Every sale is literally an all-or-nothing gamble: "They trembled especially to see [Mouret] wager all the money in his coffers on one hand of cards, to fill the various departments with mountains of merchandise without holding back a penny in reserve" (3:420). When Mouret himself "confesses" to the baron, he speaks of the "successive expansions, the profits continually reinvested in the business, . . . the store risking its existence with every new sale in which the entire capital was wagered on one hand in a card game" (3:456).

This calculated and calculating presentation of the operations involved in the department store is meant to persuade Hartmann the financier. But more fundamentally, the process described by Mouret serves to structure rhythmically the whole of the narrative. The rhythm is established by illustrating, in three equivalent scenes interspersed throughout the novel, the economic mechanisms Mouret champions. In the course of the fourteen chapters that make up *Au Bonheur des Dames,* an important sale takes place in each of three different chapters: chapters 4, 9, and 14. Once the reader is past the introductory material, he encounters sale scenes at precise, regular intervals until the novel closes. Moreover, the final chapter is itself a summation of the whole process in the form of the most spectacular sale of all, the white sale. There can be no doubt that this rhythmic presentation was carefully planned by Zola, who, as Henri Mitterand has amply demonstrated, always structured the episodes of his novels in detailed outlines before he began to write.[1] The basic rhythm of the sale scenes also contains a clearly progressive movement. Following the first sale, each new one marks an increase in profits over the preceding one until finally the fabled figure of one million francs in gross revenues for a single

day is reached in the last sale. Each sale episode serves as triumphant testimony to the proper functioning of the rules outlined by
Mouret.

An additional, secondary rhythm is introduced to drive the point
home. Interspersed between the three sales are three inventories,
although only one of them is actually described at length in the
text. The information furnished concerning the first inventory
emphasizes not only increasing profits, but also the increasing rap-
idity of turnover: "It was said that Mouret's original capital investment, the first five hundred thousand francs augmented each
year by the totality of the profits earned, a capital which was now
valued at something like four million, had been converted into
merchandise ten times [during the year] in the store's departments" (3:598). The fact that the cycle money–commodity–money has been completed ten times, as we learn in this passage, already marks a quantitative evolution in comparison with the earlier
conversation between Mouret and Hartmann, during which a yearly
turnover rate of four was mentioned. The second inventory allows
Mouret to realize that the rate of turnover has increased to twelve
instead of the previous ten. The third inventory, described at length
in chapter 10, reveals an increase of ten million francs in gross
revenues over the preceding year. Each inventory, then, is added
testimony to the smooth functioning of the speculative process.
The structure of the novel's text brings the reader regularly back
to the premises of Mouret's operation: the entire amount of capital
he possesses is invested without reserve in commodities on the occasion of each new sale, and each inventory stresses the relatively
small amount of capital involved combined with a rapidly increasing rate of turnover in the cycle money–commodity–money.

If Saccard's practice had already seriously undermined the traditional belief that wealth is accumulation (despite his ultimate
failure to destroy that belief entirely), Mouret now takes things
even further. Within the scope of his own activity, accumulation
has been transformed into a process which might more accurately
be termed expansion and which will be explored more fully shortly. With respect to the traditional practice of accumulation, Mouret
retains an attitude marked at times by nostalgia, although that

nostalgia never interferes with his transactions. He likes to see (and, one could probably add, to feel and hear) the money brought in by the business done in the store. Witness his departure from Mme Desforges's apartment following his discussion with Baron Hartmann: "They shook hands, and Mouret, appearing overjoyed, took his leave, because he did not like to dine before he had returned in the evening to take a look at the daily receipt of Au Bonheur des Dames" (3:496). Sale days in particular are occasions for sheer delight. Following the second sale, Lhomme, the chief cashier for the store, and his son carry the cash receipts up to Mouret's office.

[Mouret] was as happy as a child. The cashier and
his son put down their load. The satchel made a
clear golden ring, two of the bags burst and released
floods of silver and copper, while corners of bank
notes showed out of the wallet. A whole end of the
main desk was covered. It was as if a fortune had
fallen there, collected in the space of ten hours.
     When Lhomme and Albert had left, Mouret,
wiping off his face, remained motionless for a moment, his eyes on the money, lost in thought.
(3:645)

Thus, as was indicated at the end of the analysis of *La Curée,* gold has left the façade of the mansion on the Parc Monceau and found its way to Mouret's desk. Yet Mouret's fascination with the gold piled high on his desk never goes far enough to break the circle of exchange. For a fleeting moment he contemplates the receipts, whereupon they immediately reenter the circulational process as they return to the central treasury of the store to be exchanged anew for commodities.

Up to this point, the economic system oulined in *Au Bonheur des Dames* has been considered only in skeletal form, purely from the point of view of monetary laws. Several more complex issues must now be addressed, beginning with a fundamental difference between *Au Bonheur* and *La Curée.* In *La Curée,* Saccard's speculation involving real estate creates what one might term a "captive" buyer. The government has definite plans to renovate parts of Paris; it is sufficient for the speculator to know exactly which parts of the city are included in the renovation in order to possess the necessary property at the moment when monetary compensations for condemned areas begin to be distributed. In short, whatever happens, sale of the property acquired by the speculator is assured. The government must buy in order to push forward its projects. In fact, as we have seen, when Saccard abandons this scheme and builds on the property he has purchased in collaboration with Mignon and Charrier, he then discovers the laws of a market in which the buyer is *not* captive. At this precise point he suffers a setback in his financial affairs. In *Au Bonheur des Dames,* on the contrary, the buyer is not captive and his presence is not assured a priori. He (or perhaps we should say she, since Mouret's clientele consists mainly of women) must be captured. The success of Octave's undertaking cannot depend entirely on the purely mechanical laws of the circulation of money. It depends equally on his ability to create a pool of customers, on what we might call seduction in a wide sense. Much of *Au Bonheur* is devoted to a description of the strategies he employs to attain this goal.

First and foremost, Mouret's success hinges on his ability to assemble crowds in his store. Rapid turnover in a department store implies rapid buying that can only be produced by concentrating large numbers of people on the premises of the store. As Naomi Schor remarks, "Octave cannot take his customers for granted; if his brilliant displays, his saturation advertising, do not drive his female customers into a frenzy of spending, his grandiose schemes of expansion will surely crumble, his business possibly fail."[2] In her mention of displays and advertising, Schor hints at dynamic processes at work in the creation of the necessary crowd of customers. However, she does not really pursue this question because she is interested instead in exploring Zola's narrative technique of crowd personification. What is important for my purposes is not the narrative technique but, rather, precisely the *dynamic process* of crowd formation. Without the crowd, there could be no speculation in the form devised by Mouret. The crowd is an intrinsic dynamic component of a new economic form, and consequently, it is of utmost importance to understand the mechanisms of its formation.

Michel Serres's analyses are the most pertinent for my concerns here and provide a fertile point of departure. As Serres states initially, "Octave is a topologist."[3] In other words, Mouret's first weapon is that of space, as the narrator himself clearly reveals in the text of the novel:

> But the area in which Mouret revealed himself as a
> master without a rival was in the interior arrange-
> ment of the store. His law was that no corner of Au
> Bonheur des Dames was to remain deserted. He re-
> quired noise, crowds, life everywhere, because life,
> as he was fond of saying, attracts life: it replicates
> and spreads. He drew all sorts of applications from
> this law. First, there had to be a crush to enter the
> store; people in the street had to believe there was a
> riot. And he obtained this press at the doors by put-
> ting sale items there, racks and baskets overflowing
> with items at low prices. Thus, the more modest
> shoppers conglomerated there, barring the entrance,
> making people think that the store was absolutely
> full, when often it was only half full. (3:613–14)

Serres compares this movement at the doors of the store to the damming up of a flow which then overflows like a waterfall into the store itself.[4] The first lesson in crowd formation is that a crowd draws a crowd, or better yet, the appearance of a crowd draws a crowd.

What happens once the clientele penetrates into the store? It is channeled from counter to counter and trapped. As early as his first interview with Hartmann, Octave shows his awareness of this process:

> First, mastery was increased tenfold by piling up
> merchandise. All the merchandise was accumulated
> at one point, reinforcing itself and foisting itself off

on the buyer. There was never a moment's respite;
the item for the season was always there. And from
department to department, the client found herself
trapped, bought fabric in one place, thread further
on, a coat elsewhere, outfitted herself, and then hap-
pened upon unexpected encounters, gave in to the
need for the useless and the pretty. (3:459)

However, if such is Mouret's strategy even at this early moment,
the logic of the floor plan within the store is as yet ill-conceived.
On the eve of the second sale, Octave gives serious critical thought
to the interior arrangement of Au Bonheur for the first time: "He
had suddenly realized that the arrangement he had adopted for the
various departments was inept. And yet it was absolutely logical:
fabric on one side, ready-to-wear on the other, an intelligent order
which permitted his clients to find their way themselves" (3:614).
But this is precisely the point. If the customer is left to her own
intelligence and logic, then her buying activity will also remain
intelligent. Consequently, the frenzied, aimless movement that
Octave is attempting to provoke cannot occur.   Mouret, who af-
firmed the power of spatial arrangement in his conversation with
Hartmann, has not yet fully exploited his own discovery. As Serres
contends, "Logic . . . obliterated space. It rendered it clear. The
master has forgotten geometry, which situates the crowd. A woman enters; she goes directly where she wants to go, moves from
class to class, . . . and leaves without getting lost."[5] Octave inaugurates the second sale by destroying the logic of the store and
rendering space opaque once more: "Abruptly, he had shouted out
that the whole thing had to be destroyed" (3:614). Henceforth,
the power of space will be enlisted to its full potential in the interior of the store. Mme Marty, the archetypal victim created by
Mouret's scheme, unwittingly testifies to its success—first by
spending too much and then by remarking: "There is no order in
this store. One gets lost; one ends up doing stupid things" (3:637).

Mouret's exploitation of space is far from remaining confined
solely to the interior of his store. Very early in the text of *Au Bonheur des Dames* the narrator speaks specifically of one of the projects

for renovating the city of Paris, namely, the "extension of the Rue Réaumur, of which a new section was to be opened under the name Rue du Dix-Décembre, between the Place de la Bourse and the Place de l'Opéra" (3:455). Cognizant of this project, Mouret begins to imagine a plan for expansion that will culminate in a grand façade on the new Rue du Dix-Décembre. "Since the Rue du Dix-Décembre was supposed to intersect with the Rue de Choiseul and the Rue de la Michodière, [Mouret] imagined Au Bonheur des Dames invading the whole block bordered by these streets and the Rue Neuve-Saint-Augustin; he could already imagine the store with a palatial façade facing the new street, dominating, master of the conquered city" (3:455). I shall have more to say concerning the symbolic aspects of this passage and others in which the new street is at stake, but for the moment, suffice it to say that the construction of the street and of Mouret's cherished façade form a leitmotiv in the novel emphasizing the constant expansion of the store.

The project for the façade encounters difficulties, as was mentioned earlier, because the Crédit Immobilier owns the building needed for its construction and plans to build a hotel in the same space. This gives rise to a further discussion between Mouret and Hartmann that is extremely instructive for the present analysis. The reader should be aware that at the moment of the new meeting between the two businessmen, the Crédit Immobilier has already backed Mouret to a large extent by ceding to him almost all the property necessary for his continued expansion. In the end, only the fate of one final building remains to be negotiated. Hartmann, who has become Octave's defender in the bank's executive committees, reports back to Octave during another of Mme Desforges's afternoon gatherings. The bank is still unfavorable to the projected façade. As Hartmann puts it, "My goodness! They are saying what I told you myself, what I still believe to some extent... Your façade is only an ornament; the new construction would enlarge the surface area of your store only by one-tenth, and that's a rather large investment for something which is only an advertisement" (3:688). Hartmann's explanation draws a blistering response from Octave:

An advertisement! An advertisement! In any case, this one will be made of stone, and it will bury us all. You don't understand that our business will increase tenfold! In two years, we'll recoup our investment. What is the importance of what you call lost space, if that space pays you an enormous interest! . . . You'll see the crowd when our clientele no longer clogs up the Rue Neuve-Saint-Augustin and is able to rush in freely by means of a wide avenue in which six carriages will be able to drive with ease. (Ibid.)

We must understand clearly the utility alleged in Mouret's argument. He maintains that up to the present, free circulation providing access to his store has always been obstructed by the ancient and narrow streets of the neighborhood in which his business is located. The new boulevard will provide an artery for rapid transportation that will allow an increasing number of people to arrive unhindered at his door.[6] If one places this development within the context of the entire novel, a chiasmatic figure with respect to the treatment of space in *Au Bonheur* becomes apparent. Initially, outside the store, space is opaque, obstructed, full of accidents, while within the store itself space is clear, logical, and therefore in a sense nonexistent. We have seen how Octave transforms the interior of the store in order to maximize profits. This interior transformation is accompanied by its opposite outside the store. Inside, space becomes opaque and obstructed; outside, it becomes clear and susceptible to unhampered circulation as a result of the construction of the new boulevard. As Octave's undertaking gathers momentum, his use of space encompasses a domain even larger than the store itself. The façade, with its resulting connection to the projected thoroughfare, participates in a logic of space that permeates the search for increasing profits throughout the novel.

It is interesting to encounter the question of façades once again in the context of the preceding argument. In *La Curée* it became evident that façades were functional to a certain extent: they created an appearance of wealth necessary for the generation of credit.

However, with respect to the Saccard mansion, it was also clear that the façade could veer suddenly from the realm of speculation back into that of accumulation. In *Au Bonheur* the store façade is resolutely functional. On a first level, it is calculated to use space properly, to provide a spacious entrance facing a wide avenue, to allow customers to enter the store unhindered by outside traffic.

Yet even in its more decorative aspects it fulfills a well-defined utilitarian role: it is an advertisement, and an impressive one at that, as the baron himself is forced to admit despite his feeble objections to Octave's project. A description of the store's façade furnished later when construction is completed confirms its functionality. It is conceived in such a way as to avoid interference with the display of merchandise which is, in the end, the goal of the whole enterprise—it opens the displays to the beholder: "On the ground floor, the decoration remained sober in order not to interfere with the fabric displayed in the windows: a base of sea-green marble, the corner abutments and supporting pillars covered in black marble, the severity of which was lightened by golden scrolls. The rest was clear glass supported by iron frames, nothing but glass which seemed to open the depths of the galleries and halls to the sunlight of the street" (3:761–62). Only in its higher portions is the façade allowed fanciful variations which, due to their location, cannot distract the customer and turn her or him away from the merchandise within the store. And even in this upper portion of the architecture, utilitarian materials, such as ceramic tiles and steel, are dominant. Although the store is quite evidently related to Saccard's sumptuous mansion on the Parc Monceau, it also differs decisively, because now the beholder's gaze is allowed to penetrate fully to the "depths of the galleries and halls." The public is not to remain outside but, rather, to be drawn as deeply as possible into the maze. The façade no longer hides speculative operations behind its brilliant surface. On the contrary, it puts on display the very merchandise that must be sold to assure success. Advertisement, *advertere,* to turn toward: all eyes turn toward the store without, however, stopping at the surface. The facade in its more practical form here is both visible and invisible, attractive and self-effacing. A calculated use of the space of the new boulevard combined with the transparency of the entrance facing it allow Mouret to accomplish what originally was only a dream, namely, "[to make] the street go right through the store" (3:614).[7]

Although the linking of Mouret's store with the Rue du Dix-Décembre has until now been viewed mainly as a functional expediency, one cannot deny its emblematic dimension. For Octave, the new street represents the new Paris, and he explicitly contrasts the new city with the old. Until he can connect his own business with a part of the new city, he will always feel left out of the modern society that he sees forming in the wake of the Second Empire. "As long as the main entrance was on the Rue Neuve-Saint-Augustin, in a dark street of the old Paris, his work would remain crippled, illogical. He wanted it to be visible in the eyes of the new Paris, on one of the young avenues where the throng of the century's end rode by in the bright sunlight" (3:687). Mouret's desire symbolically marks his attachment to the Second Empire as that society which has permitted the rise of his own speculative venture. It is particularly significant that Octave expresses his faith in the empire through the act of joining his store with one of the new streets of the city.

The importance of Haussmann's undertakings as the basis for Aristide Saccard's speculation in *La Curée* has already been made clear. *Au Bonheur des Dames* marks a new encounter with the renovation of Paris and inserts Mouret into a paradigm already including Napoleon III and Saccard. It was suggested earlier that a strong narcissistic component reinforces the emperor's and Saccard's desires to reshape the city in their own image. Octave's own project clearly utilizes and benefits from the network of boulevards in a similar manner. They give him access to more potential customers who can be led into the spatial trap laid for them inside Au Bonheur. The boulevards will permit Mouret to impose his will on the city as never before, to reshape it in his own way by turning it into a vast reservoir of buyers at his mercy. "There was an ever-widening circle, an effulgence of the clientele drawn in from the four corners of the city, emptying the store with the roaring din of a floodgate" (3:799). Moreover, Octave and Napoleon III are related in an even more precise sense by a specific talent they share:

both are masters at controlling crowds. In Napoleon III's projects, the renovations give access to hidden pockets of Paris, thereby allowing the army and the police to penetrate those recesses and prevent popular uprisings that thrive only when communications among the forces of repression are difficult. As one historian puts it, "By destroying narrow streets well-adapted to barricades and by placing imposing barracks from which straight avenues radiated out—apparently propitious for artillery fire or cavalry charges—[Napoleon III and Haussmann] might well have been taking into consideration problems relating to public order, haunted as they were by recent memories."[8] The control of crowds, especially Parisian crowds, is one of the major premises of Napoleon III's political power. As Théodore Gilquin's activities in helping to create the empire demonstrate, the formative moments of Bonapartism required the manipulation of crowds by the use of republican rhetoric in working-class cafés. Later, the capture of Plassans depicted in *La Fortune des Rougon* demonstrates yet another successful mob operation, directed in this instance against the anti-Bonapartist revolt.

The mob is equally essential to Mouret's own project. Without it, his commercial venture could not exist. His whole spatial strategy is devoted to provoking it, entrapping it, and directing its frenzy toward profitable ends. It is fitting, therefore, that Octave's connection to the Second Empire should occur via the Rue du Dix-Décembre and that he should envisage the new street in terms of manipulating the crowd of customers. The very name of the street is highly significant in this context, because it commemorates Napoleon III's first great public victory, achieved with the help of the masses on the occasion of his election to the presidency, namely, on 10 December 1848. Moreover, the reader may recall that the Bonapartist loyalists, Marx's *Lumpenproletariat,* the crowd that Bonaparte excelled in manipulating, were organized by Bonaparte and his supporters into a semipolitical, paramilitary organization called, appropriately enough, the Société du Dix Décembre. This organization was the focus of some of Marx's most scorching verbal flourishes in *The Eighteenth Brumaire,* one of which bears quoting here:

What the National Workshops were for the socialist
workers, what the Mobile Guard was for the bourgeois republicans, the Society of 10 December was
for Bonaparte: the characteristic fighting force of his
party. On his journeys detachments of the Society
had to pack the trains and improvise a public for
him, had to stage public enthusiasm, scream the
words *vive l'empereur,* insult and beat up republicans,
all with the protection of the police, of course.
When he returned to Paris they had to form the advance guard, and forestall or disperse counter-dem-
onstrations. . . . The history of the Society of 10
December is his own history.[9]

The similarities between Napoleon III's political undertaking and
Octave's speculative enterprise could not be more strikingly emphasized than by means of a street bearing the name Dix-Décembre. A final note in the analysis of the symbolic significance of
this street warrants mention: the rue du Dix-Décembre runs between the stock exchange and the opera. One need only follow it
to arrive at the locus of Zola's third novel concerning speculation,
namely, the stock exchange in *L'Argent,* which is thus linked to
the Second Empire by the very same topographical device.

We are not yet ready, however, to stroll down the rue du Dix-
Décembre to the stock exchange. Other aspects of Octave's venture remain to be analyzed. In order to mobilize his topographical
manipulations, Mouret must first draw a certain number of customers to his store by virtue of what he offers to sell, that is, by
virtue of the merchandise on hand. Thus his enterprise involves
not only monetary and topographical laws, but also the commodity that is to be sold, the material object at the heart of his en-
deavors. The previous analysis of *La Curée* began by focusing on
Saccard's manipulations aimed at turning his real estate holdings
into paper goods in order to circulate them unhindered by the material solidity of actual buildings. In sum, speculation implies an
approach to the commodity that tends to reduce and obscure its
use value, its material qualities. If Mouret's speculation is to be
successful, then he too must find a solution to the problem of the

commodity. Not surprisingly, he does in fact propose a new solution to the problem in the form of a twofold strategy. In the first
place, he attempts *to fragment the commodity* to an ever-increasing
extent. He does so by eschewing specialization and selling as great
a variety of objects as possible in Au Bonheur. The expansion of
the store always implies not simply an increase in space, but a con-
comitant widening of the range of objects offered for sale. Second,
despite the variety of merchandise offered by Octave, the commodities in the store nevertheless belong to a particular and significant class of objects, namely, fashion items. This type of commodity possesses certain characteristics which make it ideal for
Mouret's operations.

Let us first analyze the fragmentation of the commodity. There
are two reasons behind the drive for fragmentation through increasing variety. Octave must try to reach as many different sectors
of the population as possible. Specialized departments within the
store have the effect of bringing in well-defined groups of customers, whereupon the carefully calculated spatial arrangements
"encourage" them to purchase articles they had not originally
planned to buy. Because space within the store is confusing, it is
difficult for the customer to confine his or her interest to the specialty which initially tempted him or her. Numerous references in
the novel attest to Mouret's practice of creating departments to
attract specialized sectors of prospective customers. One might take
as an example the first sale in chapter 4, which is highlighted by
an exposition of Turkish rugs with explicit strategic goals.
"[Mouret] was the first to buy a collection of old and new rugs from
sources in the Middle East under excellent conditions, rugs of the
rare type which only curiosity shops had carried until then and
sold at very high prices. And he planned to flood the market with
them; he sold them nearly at cost, using them simply as a splendid
decor which would draw the sophisticated artistic clientele into
his store" (3:471). The same kind of operation occurs repeatedly
throughout the novel, whether it be by opening a department for
umbrellas or by opening one for children's clothes in order to
"conquer the mother through her child" (3:612). The narrator puts
it aptly when he states that Mouret "speculated on all feelings"

(ibid.), from the esthetic sensitivity of the "sophisticated artistic clientele" down to maternal instincts of the everyday shopper.

The second motivation behind the search for increasing fragmentation of the commodity through variety is related to the rules of monetary circulation. The greater the variety of merchandise offered, the smaller the risk incurred by the failure to sell any one particular item. Octave cannot hope that every commodity he stocks will enjoy equal success. Variety will allow him to lower the price of unsuccessful items in order to sell them off at a loss while recouping that loss in other departments. Merchandise that cannot be sold at a profit does not thereby hinder the process of rapid circulation at the heart of Mouret's project. Blockages that could occur as a result of large concentrations of capital in one particular area (for example, real estate holdings in *La Curée*) are effectively prevented. The ability to regulate prices over the whole domain of the department store is not simply a preventive ploy, however; it is also a competitive one. The passage quoted in the preceding paragraph already hinted at this possibility. To inundate the market with Turkish rugs sold at cost not only draws a certain group of customers, but deals a death blow to specialty stores that carry only Turkish rugs and survive by selling them at high prices. Fragmentation and variety in the commodities sold combined with the avowed objective of rapid turnover allow Mouret to enter into price wars with competing shops and to destroy all the smaller competitors in the neighborhood surrounding his department store. Finally, purposefully lowering the price of a popular item below the profit-making level can function as a further inducement to customers, because the item can then become the focus of the advertisement for money-saving bargains. The customer succumbs to the temptation presented by a loss leader, is subsequently entrapped within the store, and uncontrollably spends money elsewhere. "We lose a few cents on the item, I agree. So what? That's a welcome misfortune if we thereby draw in all the women and have them at our mercy, seduced, distracted amongst the piles of our other merchandise, emptying their purses without counting!" (3:425) explains Mouret at one point.

But fragmentation is only one means of attempting to dissipate the materiality of the commodity in order to facilitate circulation and increase turnover. Mouret's efforts simultaneously go in a second direction that can best be analyzed by an approach which takes the generic name of Octave's enterprise as its point of departure. Octave is engaged in what is termed in French "le commerce de nouveautés." The *Robert* gives the following definition of the word *nouveauté* used in this context: "new production of the fashion industry." *Mode,* in turn, is defined as "collective and passing habits with respect to clothing." Now, Octave has built his empire by dealing in a very specific type of commodity—the fashion item. The two characteristics of fashion given in the *Robert* definition reveal clearly why Mouret has chosen this particular type of commodity. First, fashion amounts to "collective habits." It is a domain in which the freedom of the individual subject is effectively negated. When the subject enters the realm of fashion, his desires and needs are determined by a "collective other," by a group of people whose behavior and appearance dictate his own; he becomes an anonymous member of the crowd that throngs through Mouret's store. The individual subject never buys a given fashion commodity for its intrinsic concrete worth or usefulness, but only because that commodity has been designated as desirable by the other.

In the realm of fashion, we are always dealing with a triangular schema: the subject, the commodity, and the other. The triangular structure of desire has been the focal point of René Girard's work since the publication of *Deceit, Desire, and the Novel.* Girard contends that desire never reaches out for the object in a direct and uncomplicated way, but always passes through a mediator/model/rival who must first designate the object as desirable for it to become so. Nowhere is this structure played out as explicitly as in the domain of fashion commodities. A market economy seems to be able to take hold of the mimetic phenomena associated with triangular desire (which Girard more recently refers to as the mimesis of appropriation)[10] and use it to drive the process of exchange. As Girard notes, "What capitalism does, or rather the liberal society which permits capitalism to develop, is to assure a freer play of mimetic phenomena and their channeling towards economic and technological activities."[11] Octave's enterprise could easily be viewed as the knowledgeable exploitation of mimetic desire within an exchange economy. The process of triangular desire propels the circulational structure established by Mouret, and vice versa, in a positive feedback circuit that can lead only to ever-increasing expansion. [12]

The articulation between the mimesis of appropriation and the economic domain may be explored in more precise terms with the help of an essay by Jean-Pierre Dupuy entitled "Le Signe et l'envie."[13] Dupuy accepts the Girardian thesis that the fundamental structure of mimesis is triangular. An individual desires an object because it has been marked as desirable by a second individual who serves as a model for the first. There is no spontaneous desire, no spontaneous reaching for the object: desire is always mediated. Moreover, the designated object is unique; no other object can take its place. As Girard remarks, "In the eyes of the desirer, other objects have no value, even though they may be similar to or indeed identical with the 'mediated' object."[14] Dupuy notes, however, that the objects at stake in Girard's *Deceit, Desire, and the Novel* and in the works of the novelists studied therein are of a particular type: "a person from whom one wants a service, recognition, friendship, love, or a possession; an event in which one wants to play a particular role; a place one desires to inhabit, possess, conquer; a quality, a distinction one wants to acquire" ("Signe," p. 112). Indeed, such objects can be thought of only in terms of all or nothing: they cannot be shared nor can anything be substituted in their place. However, the uniqueness of these objects is due not only to the focusing power of the structure of mimetic desire; it is also related to the nature of the objects themselves: "If that uniqueness is related in part to the extraordinary properties of mimetic desire, it is also related to the very nature of the object at stake" (ibid.).

An analysis of specifically economic objects reveals that they differ in kind from the types of objects upon which Girard concentrates. In particular, the economic object is one that has been transformed into a commodity in the Marxist sense, or, as Dupuy contends, "It only has value, it only exists as a result of its relationship to other objects for which one can always exchange it" ("Signe," p. 113). Dupuy continues: "The abstract logic of equivalence and of exchange value seems to be in total opposition to the logic of the mimesis of appropriation. Out of objects that are 'priceless' for their possessor, the logic of exchange creates merchandise commensurable with any exchange value that lingers about the public places of the consumer society" (ibid.). If such be the case, then the violence that can result from a direct confrontation between mimetic rivals, at least with respect to commodities, is avoided. If the subject's mediator designates a particular economic object as desirable, the desiring individual can obtain the same object or any number of its equivalents in the marketplace, where everything is a commodity and is therefore exchangeable. Thus, one could say that while a market economy greatly expands the domain in which the phenomena associated with the mimesis of appropriation are rife, at the same time it decreases the potentiality for violent confrontations by diverting energies into the circuit of economic exchange, where the possibility of endless substitutions defuses conflicts among individual desires.

Is this combination of mimetic and economic behavior not the very basis of the fashion business? What, then, are the implications with respect to the commodity itself? In yet another way, its actual use value, its material characteristics, become secondary to its symbolic significance. The purchase of a fashion item is dictated by the other or group of others and situates the individual with respect to that other. Utilitarian considerations are secondary at best. Once again, as in *La Curée*, though in a rather different way this time, the commodity involved in the speculative venture loses its concrete existence to become a mere signifier. No longer desired as the result of any spontaneous individual need, it becomes instead the signifier of membership in the collective other that has become the source of desire.

The passages in the text of *Au Bonheur des Dames* that mark the loss of individuality on the part of those who enter into the store are numerous. One could take, for example, the entrance scene at the beginning of Octave's second sale.

> Swept up by the current, the women could not turn
> back. . . . They could move forward only very

slowly, squeezed together so tightly they could
hardly breathe, held upright by shoulders and abdo-
mens, whose soft warmth they could feel. And their
satiated desire took pleasure in this difficult approach, which stimulated their curiosity even more.
It was a chaotic mixture of women dressed in silk,
petit bourgeois women in cheap dresses, hatless
girls, all whipped into a frenzy by the same passion.
(3:618)

Naomi Schor has said of this passage, "The text reads like a dem-
onstration of the painful process whereby an individual divests
himself of his highly prized difference and autonomy to become a
(mere) part of the collective."[15] The physical forcing together of
so many bodies transforms them into one. Also evident here is the
relation between the dynamics of crowd formation itself and the
idea of fashion. Fashion necessarily implies mediation by a collective other *that easily assumes the form of a crowd.* Mouret assembles
that crowd in order to tap the potential of the fashion mechanism
within his store. Nothing is to be left to chance. The assembling
of a crowd around a particular item can work almost like a chem-
ical reaction that instantaneously creates a fashion. Such is the case
for the "Paris-Bonheur" silk that is the promotional item of the
first sale staged by Octave. It becomes the focus of the sale's success: "Meanwhile, the overcrowding in the silk department was
becoming such that Mme Desfarges and Mme Marty at first could
not find a salesman who was free. . . . But a great success was
especially evident for the Paris-Bonheur silk, around which a wave
of infatuation was growing, one of those unexpected fevers which
establishes a style in one day" (3:488). To bring together a crowd
and a highly advertised fashion item is a necessary and nearly sufficient condition for creating a new fashion.

If one creates an area in which the customer abdicates his individuality and hears only the voice of the other, the fundamental
strategic position to be occupied by the speculator is precisely that
of the collective other. The perspicacious retailer of fashion items
does not simply leave the formation of fashion trends to the collective group of customers, but instead attempts to assume the

voice of the collective other that dictates those trends. As Theodor Adorno puts it so aptly: "The abundance of commodities indiscriminately consumed is becoming calamitous. It makes it impossible to find one's way, and just as in a gigantic department store one looks for a guide, the population wedged between wares await their leader."[16] The success of Au Bonheur logically leads to an unprecedented explosion of advertising techniques.

> His great strength lay especially in the domain of advertising. Mouret had gotten to the point where he was spending three hundred thousand francs a year on catalogues, notices, and posters. For the summer fashion sale he had distributed two hundred thousand catalogues, fifty thousand of which had gone to foreign countries translated into all sorts of languages. Now he was illustrating them with prints and even including samples glued to the pages. The store's displays were overflowing, Au Bonheur des Dames was becoming visible throughout the world, invading walls, newspapers, even curtains in theaters. (3:613)

In fact, one of Mouret's specific and most powerful talents is his ability to arrange displays of merchandise in the most striking manner, to suggest the fashionable and desirable qualities of merchandise by proper combinations of color and form. "Everyone agreed, the owner was the best display creator in Paris, a revolutionary decorator in reality, who had founded the school of the brutal and the colossal in the science of displays" (3:434). Nothing must be left to chance: pleasing displays of the commodities within the store amount to suggestions as to the desirability of those commodities. Indications of Mouret's talent in this area are numerous in the novel's text and culminate in the great exposition of white that highlights the inauguration of the store's new façade in the final chapter.

Mouret's flair for the art of arranging objects and colors signals his mastery of signs and brings him closer to the figure of Saccard. Aristide is accomplished in the literary domain, Octave in the domain of the plastic arts. Their respective styles, however, are not that different. The operative words in Mouret's case are "brutal" and "colossal." His creations rise up to shock and provoke the beholder. [17] Much the same could be said of Saccard, whose style, we have seen, tends toward the melodramatic. No subtleties or drawing-room comedies for him but, rather, plots that feature sudden reversals and complications that seem too obvious and contrived to be believed. The works of both Mouret and Saccard stand out and are effective precisely because they are provocative. Moreover, Mouret is a Saccard-like figure in another way as well: he too is an accomplished actor. His success with his feminine clientele is due to a seductive role he invariably assumes when speaking *ex cathedra* as head of Au Bonheur. Illustration of this fact is provided early in the novel, during the first discussion between Hartmann and Octave. As the two talk, the group of women gathered in Mme Desforges's salon are discussing Au Bonheur and finally call Mouret to ask for information concerning the coming sale. He is clearly irritated by the interruption. However, when he realizes he must respond, his disposition changes almost instantaneously: "Finally, he relented and with an apparent good grace, an appearance of delight at which the baron marveled" (3:462). Octave's face assumes an appearance, "un air," which belies his underlying anger: he too possesses his mask for official occasions. The very tone of voice he employs is an artifice: "a flute-like voice, an actor's voice which he assumed when he spoke with women" (ibid.).

The abdication of the customers when faced with the will of the other permeates the relationship between salesperson and customer. Once within the store, the salesperson's word gains almost unquestioned authority. Class rules are as if reversed. Generally, those hired to do the selling in Mouret's store are taken from the lower classes, whereas the clients are from the bourgeoisie or upper bourgeoisie. Nevertheless, the salesperson occupies the position of the other within the confines of the store and thus reigns supreme. A striking example is furnished by Mme Marty, who, as has already been suggested, serves as the most typical representative of the store's customers. Mme Marty attempts to buy a coat for her daughter in one scene of the novel and submits to the authority of Marguerite, a saleswoman who works with the novel's heroine,

Denise. "When [Marguerite] heard Mme Marty say that she did not want to spend more than two hundred francs, her face took on an expression of pity. Oh! Madame would go higher than that, it would be impossible for madame to find anything suitable for two hundred francs. And she threw the more ordinary coats on the counter with a gesture that signified: 'Look at that. What poor quality!' Mme Marty dared not disagree" (3:496). A further development along these same lines occurs when Octave allows hawkers to work within the store. "Mouret used hawking, items offered for sale by criers, the clientele buttonholed and cleaned out" (3:620). While certain of Mouret's competitors avoid this kind of selling, on the pretext that "merchandise [should speak] for itself" (ibid.), Octave has understood that in the domain of fashion, it is not the commodities that speak but, rather, the voice of a collective other. One is always well-advised to assume such a powerful position oneself instead of leaving it to someone else.

A word of caution is in order here. The analysis of the mechanisms used by Octave to obscure the materiality of the commodity might have given the impression of total dominance on his part. Such is not always the case: there are moments when the turnover process is rather rudely interrupted. During the description of the inventory in chapter 10 of *Au Bonheur,* the reader learns that Bouthemont, who is in charge of the fabric department of the store, bought too much printed silk for the summer season and is left with an overstock at the moment of accounting: "And the call for printed silk was never-ending. Under his breath, Favier pointed out that the leftover stock would be considerable: the management was going to be happy. That foolish Bouthemont was perhaps the premier Parisian buyer, but as a salesman he'd never seen such an idiot" (3:661). Miscalculation is possible: one may unite all the conditions that supposedly trigger the formation of a fashion and yet fail. In a business that must exploit fashion, the inability to foresee trends and to help create them is a mortal sin, as it were, punishable by the quick demise of the party guilty of such a shortcoming. Thus Bouthemont's days are numbered: "Indeed, his position at Au Bonheur des Dames was threatened since the last inventory. As hard as he tried to blame the rainy season, he was not

pardoned for the considerable remaining stock of printed silk. . . .
Mouret had condemned him" (3:678–79).

Despite Octave's complex system, the materiality of the commodity can suddenly reappear inopportunely in the midst of his
activities and cause serious disruptions. His attempts to skirt the
materiality of the commodity are in many ways more viable than
were Saccard's in *La Curée*. He has found ways of greatly increasing
the speed of the circulational process by multiplying the turnover,
and he has reduced the dangers involved in single, concentrated
investments by fragmenting the object of investment. Yet blockages can still occur, as the Bouthemont episode suggests, and they
remind us that the total disappearance of the commodity's materiality is a theoretical limit that will always remain unattainable
in practice. A closer approach to that theoretical limit will occur
in *L'Argent,* a novel in which speculation reaches its culminating
form and in which the process we have been tracing attains its
developmental limit.

It is interesting and significant that threats to the smooth operation of *Au Bonheur* twice occur in the form of bad weather:
Bouthemont's miscalculation but also the disaster that nearly be-
falls Mouret on the occasion of the first sale, described in chapter
4. On the morning of the sale, Mouret tours the store only to discover that it is nearly empty. The customers upon whom he has
counted are not present. "He was slightly pale, his eyes clear and
resolute nonetheless. In making his rounds of the departments, he
had found them empty, and the possibility of a defeat had abruptly presented itself, in the midst of his stubborn faith in his own
fortune" (3:477). Later in the day, customers finally arrive, and
the sale becomes a success. The slow beginning is attributed to
weather conditions: "The disastrous morning, undoubtedly due to
a shower which had occurred around nine o'clock, could still be
reversed, because the blue sky of the morning had taken on a gay
air of victory" (3:482). One can go only so far in the suppression
of the material aspects in the process of economic circulation. The
fact that they can crop up in their most elementary ("the elements") and primordial form is a direct, almost brutal reminder
of their presence and of the theoretical limits of Mouret's under-

The Play of Fashion

taking. If heavy rain ever coincided with a sale day, a serious blow might be inflicted upon Mouret's enterprise because the financial margin of error is so slight.

I have discussed the first part of the *Robert* definition of fashion as "collective habits." But there is also a second characteristic of those habits, namely, the fact that they are passing, fleeting. Since the essence of the fashion commodity is not its material use value, but rather its power to signify, the possibility is left open for an infinite renewal of that process of signification. The most fashionable item is always the latest. In a sense, fashion develops by setting itself off from itself. The vanguard aspect of this movement is just as intimately a function of fashion as is the perhaps more familiar mass rush toward participation that occurs once a particular fashion has succeeded. There are really only two possible reactions toward fashion: to follow it or to set oneself off from it. One cannot escape from it, however, because both types of reaction are clearly governed by it. Moreover, one reaction drives the other, and vice versa, in a positive feedback process that seems characteristic of the fashion domain.

Fashion is fleeting because it provokes constant renewal, and as such, it is a perfect vehicle for Mouret's undertaking. Could one find a group of commodities better suited to increasing the speed of turnover in a selling operation? In addition, although Mouret constantly attempts to expand his clientele, he can always be certain of retaining the original clientele, because, by definition, there is no saturation point with respect to fashion. New and different items are constantly being created; those who have bought will return to buy again. The retention as well as the renewal of the clientele is an important issue and is indeed the first question raised by Hartmann when Octave develops his ideas on stores in chapter 3 of *Au Bonheur:* "Where will you find the clientele to fill such a cathedral?" (3:457). From the narrative point of view, the conversation with Hartmann is constructed such that Mouret's response is easy. While the two men talk, they have withdrawn from the other guests (all women and all customers of Au Bonheur des Dames) in order to have privacy, but they are able to continue to observe those other guests. Periodically, Hartmann's and Mouret's discussion is interrupted by the narrator, who shifts the reader's attention back to the other guests. The women in Mme Desforges's salon are immersed in a discussion of their own, centered precisely on the newest fashions. The baron's objections concerning customers are laid to rest by Octave's simple gesture, "The clientele, why, there it is!" Fashion creates a clientele that is in a sense always new, always ready to be carried forward by the ever-changing nature of new trends, always expanding and encompassing a widening segment of society.

The problem of the clientele raises the further question of why the target of the whole speculative process in *Au Bonheur des Dames* is invariably feminine. The connection between women and fashion is a traditional one, but it must not for that reason remain unanalyzed. In fact, it assumes a particular form in the present novel. On a fundamental level, women are portrayed as removed from the productive sphere of the economy. Witness the following passage:

> The competition among stores was a struggle for the woman, whom they continually caught in the trap of their sales after having made her dizzy with their displays. They had awakened new desires in her flesh, they were an immense temptation to which she unavoidably succumbed. She would first give in to make household purchases; then she would be taken in by coquetry and ultimately devoured. By increasing sales tenfold, by democratizing luxury, they had become a terrible source of spending, destroying families, marching to the beat of fashion's folly, always more expensive. (3:461)

There is an explicit progression in this text. The only productive function exercised by women, it suggests, is that of maintaining the home. The household purchases, however, are merely a pretext by which to draw women into the store. What Mouret and his competitors really seek to do is to go beyond the level of the household, to exploit and develop the nonproductive aspects of the woman, her desire for finery. Every cent produced by the working members of the household is thus accounted for. First, the necessities are purchased; then any remaining money is siphoned off for frivolities, that is, for fashion commodities. Finally, having thus entrapped the woman in a swirl of changing fashion, the stores provoke an increasing neglect of necessary commodities in favor of fashion items: "The stores . . . destroyed families." Mme Marty again furnishes the most complete illustration of the process by ruining her husband and then starting in on the fortune of a sympathetic and unsuspecting uncle. The senseless spending provoked by Au Bonheur brings its customers into the sphere of aimless consumption governed in the end by the frightening figure of Nana.

In his comments on Thorstein Veblen's theory of conspicuous consumption, Theodor Adorno suggests that Veblen viewed women's removal from the sphere of economic competition in the nineteenth century as a situation that may well have contained a positive potentiality. However, that potentiality never came to fruition because of women's ultimate weakened position of dependence and lack of social power:

> The state of dependence to which she is confined
> mutilates her. This counterbalances the opportunity
> offered her by her exclusion from economic competi-
> tion. Measured against the man's sphere of intellec-
> tual interests, even that of those men absorbed in
> the barbarism of business, most women find them-
> selves in a mental state which Veblen does not hesi-
> tate to term imbecilic. Following this line of
> thought, one might reach the conclusion that wom-
> en have escaped the sphere of production only to be
> absorbed all the more entirely by the sphere of con-
> sumption, to be captivated by the immediacy of the
> commodity world no less than men are transfixed by
> the immediacy of profit. Women mirror the injus-
> tice masculine society has inflicted on them—they
> become increasingly like commodities.[18]

The implication is that it was not a blessing for women to be excluded from economic competition but, rather, another and perhaps a more effective form of social bondage, one that Mouret and his competitors exploit to the fullest.

Baron Hartmann's question, "Where will you find the clientele?" contains within it not only the problem of the customer as woman, but also the question of expansion. Earlier it was suggested that traditional simple accumulation of gold gives way, in the domain of Octave's activities, to constant expansion. A venture such as his, in which all profits are immediately reinvested in the enterprise, leads logically to a continuing process of expansion. Although Mouret has discovered a way of retaining his original customers, namely, by selling a self-renewing type of commodity, nevertheless in order to avoid stagnation, he must find ever more new buyers. From his section of Paris he must branch out to the whole city: "As rivers draw toward themselves the wandering waters of the valley, it seemed as if the flow of clients, running through the entrance, soaked up the passersby from the street, sucked the population from the four corners of Paris" (3:618). Next he reaches out to the provinces to draw upon a group represented by Mme Boutarel. "She was a forty-five-year-old woman who came to Paris from time to time from the depths of some lost province. For months she would save all her pennies. Then, barely having gotten off the train, she would go to Au Bonheur des Dames, where she would spend everything" (3:475). Even this is insufficient, and Mouret finishes by organizing a mail-order service that soon overflows the borders of France itself. "This service was the one that daily was taking on the most considerable importance. . . . Orders from all over Europe rushed in; a special wagon from the post office was necessary to deliver all the correspondence" (3:709–10).

This description of expansion, limited in the present novel to the sector of fashion commodities, faithfully reproduces the program of capitalist expansion in general. The saturation of one market leads inevitably to stagnation and collapse unless a new market is discovered and developed. In a paradoxical way, capitalism always presupposes an "outside" of capitalism that can be exploited and conquered.[19] Thus, the expansive movement sooner or later must break out of national boundaries, just as Octave's commercial enterprise does. Speaking of the second half of the nineteenth century, Hannah Arendt remarks, "When capitalism had pervaded the entire economic structure and all social strata had come into the orbit of its production and consumption system, capitalists clearly had to decide either to see the whole system collapse or to find new markets."[20] The expansion of the capitalist process beyond national boundaries brings with it the political development that is commonly called imperialism and that Rosa Luxemburg defines as "the political expression of the accumulation of capital in its competitive struggle for what remains still open of the non-capitalist environment."[21] It is not surprising, therefore, that the representation of speculation in the three novels by Zola that we are studying reaches in *L'Argent*, the final novel, the stage in which what is to be sold amounts to the riches lying idle in the countries of the Middle East. From Paris in *La Curée*, economic activity branches out to the provinces and to the European countries in *Au Bonheur* to culminate in a kind of incipient imperialist development of the Middle East in *L'Argent*. Such will be the final refinement of speculation as described in the *Rougon-Macquart* cycle.

5. Taking Stock: *L'Argent*

Saccard Reborn

As in *La Curée* and *Au Bonheur des Dames,* the speculative project described in *L'Argent* is once again explicitly linked to the Second Empire. The chronology of the growth of Saccard's brainchild, the Banque Universelle, coincides with institutional history on a national scale. In the narrator's description, the zenith of the empire is reached at the moment when the World's Fair (*Exposition Universelle*) begins in Paris: "The World's Fair of 1867 opened on April 1 in the midst of celebrations, with a triumphant ostentation. The grand season of the empire was beginning" (5:228). At precisely the same moment the Banque Universelle opens the doors of its sumptuous new headquarters and inaugurates its most successful period of existence. "And it was during the same period, fifteen days later, that Saccard inaugurated the monumental building he had wanted in order to house the Universelle in a royal manner" (ibid.). The link between the empire and the bank is foregrounded in these two short passages by a coincidence of dates, but also by parallel grammatical structures (in the French version, "ce fut . . .") and by a play upon the word *universelle.* In fact, Zola is so intent upon establishing a connection between the empire and the bank that he permits a patent anachronism to subsist in the text of the novel. Established in 1864, the

Banque Universelle undergoes a development that results in a continuous rise in the value of its stock shares spanning the period from the fall of 1864 to the end of December 1867. The first and fatal decline in the value of the Universelle's stock shares occurs in January 1868. From a purely historical point of view, the sustained increase in the value of Universelle shares over the three-year period mentioned above is an impossibility. It is a well-documented fact that 1866 was a year of financial crisis in France, a crisis that began with a stock market crash especially devastating for banking institutions.[1] The financial crisis of 1866 is conspicuously absent from the text of *L'Argent,* a historical inaccuracy that serves a clear fictional purpose: it helps emphasize the crucial link between the empire and Saccard's bank. Zola manipulates history to construct a narrative sequence in which bank and empire rise concurrently to a common pinnacle and in which the collapse of the bank is a forerunner to the collapse of the empire.[2]

The relationship between Saccard's speculative project and the Second Empire goes even deeper, however, since *L'Argent* must be considered the culminating link in the series of economic novels spanning the *Rougon-Macquart* and revealing the mechanisms of speculation at work within the empire's new economic order. Let us recall briefly the definition of speculation that furnished our point of departure. Speculation was viewed as an attempt to transform the productive exchange process, represented by the cycle commodity–money–commodity, into a specular process, represented by the cycle money–commodity–money. This new cycle was the locus of an increasingly rapid turnover that required certain strategies to skirt the materiality of the commodity. However, the ruses employed always remained to some extent imperfect, since deeds were in the end actually attached to the inconveniently substantial property they represented, and the fashion merchant could not always guarantee the successful outcome of his attempt to create trends. Enter a reborn Aristide Saccard in *L'Argent* who introduces new and striking twists into the entire problematic. He will attempt to associate the public with his new speculative venture to an extent unheard of previously, the better to manipulate more thoroughly than ever before a public avid for financial adventures.

In addition, he will find a means of dispensing nearly entirely with the material commodity, of operating in a domain of extreme abstractness. Thus the evolution in the economics of the empire as Zola describes it in the *Rougon-Macquart* will be pushed to its logical conclusion in preparation for the violent conflagration that will end the imperial adventure abruptly in *La Débâcle*.

The financial undertaking recounted in *L'Argent* is the creation of a bank, the Banque Universelle. The idea for its foundation is born as a result of Saccard's encounter with Caroline and Georges Hamelin. Aristide discovers that Hamelin is an engineer who has outlined a number of projects for the economic development of the Mediterranean countries of the Middle East. First among the plans formulated by Hamelin is the creation of a maritime transportation network that would link all the countries on the shores of the Mediterranean and replace the existing, inefficient shipping lines. Hamelin's dreams spark Saccard's own dreams and lead to the conception of a bank that would finance the economic development of the region: "The exploitation of the portfolio, the implementing of the whole enormous series of projects was definitively decided. The first order of business would be the creation of a modest investment bank to underwrite the first transactions" (5:80). Saccard is faced with the pivotal problem of raising the money necessary to finance his creation. He himself does not possess the required funds, being "broke," as the narrator puts it (5:16), after his "recent and disastrous real estate deal" (5:49).

The search for the essential capital breaks naturally into two phases. First Saccard must assemble a small group of backers to buy up most of the first issue of the bank's stock shares in order to insure that none will remain unsold. These must be hardened speculators (Daigremont), men with respectable names (Bohain), or legislators capable of winning some government support for the project (Huret, for example). This original group has experience in financial affairs, and its members are enlisted as equals of Saccard, privy to any inside maneuvering that might take place. In fact, in order to persuade the group of backers to support him, Saccard is forced into an original manipulation that consists in offering them a discount on the shares they purchase. This is but the first step, however, for another portion of the founding capital must come from small investors. As Mazaud, one of Saccard's broker friends, has already declared, "But it's the number that counts... In reality, our best companies, the very foundation of the economy, are made up of modest speculators, of the great anonymous crowd who speculate" (5:89). The second step for Saccard, then, is to sell shares in his bank to numerous smaller investors, to enlist their support and associate them with his project.

But what, in fact, is Saccard selling? The stock shares offered provide the holder with an interest in the profits generated by the bank. The investors seek no commodity in the traditional sense; they desire no material object with a particular use value. Rather, to provide a first approximation of the speculative process to which the bank gives rise, one could say that they provide money to receive money in return in the form of dividends. They are, in other words, intent upon buying money itself. Thus the whole question of the commodity, requiring complicated strategies in *La Curée* and *Au Bonheur,* is short-circuited here from the very beginning. The grandiose economic investments described in the brochures for the Banque Universelle as designed to improve the quality of life in the countries involved are not what captivates the public— with one significant exception. The fundamental act at stake, buying money with money, is symbolized by what at first appears to be a very minor part of Hamelin's portfolio of engineering projects: the Société des Mines d'Argent du Carmel, the Carmel Silver Mining Company. Only limited profits can be expected from the actual practical exploitation of the mine, "a mere several million to be earned along the way" (5:75). What Saccard realizes, however, is that the hard profits do not really count; the essence is *the idea itself.* Could there be a more appealing thought than investing in a corporation that creates money by simply digging it out of the ground? Such an idea plays directly on the hopes of the smaller investors, who view their participation in the Banque Universelle as the production of money with money. The silver mine would be "an excellent advertising operation, because the idea of a silver mine, of money discovered in the ground and dug up with a shovel, was always exciting for the public, especially when one could attach a sign with a prestigious and resounding name to it—like the name Carmel" (5:75).[3] The progressively increasing importance of advertisement and publicity begins at the bank's founding moment as Saccard exploits the confusion in French between *argent* as metal and as money. What lies beneath the earth is but an inert metal—only the labor of extraction and refinement can transform it into money. Aristide's advertising campaign, however, sublimates the labor investment involved in order to create the impression that the *argent* is in its money form from the outset, that the mine is a veritable well of currency waiting to be thrown into circulation and to return to the bank's investors.

Aristide's calculation concerning the effect of the silver mine proves quite correct. Although the reader hears nothing more of it on the occasion of the first stockholders' meeting during which the bank is created, it comes quickly to the forefront when a second meeting of shareholders is called some months later to approve a project designed to double the bank's capital assets. Saccard gives the mine a prominent place in his report to the stockholders and produces the expected reaction: "As far as the Carmel silver mines were concerned, they were received with a religious electricity. And when the meeting of stockholders broke up, with a vote of thanks to the president, the director, and the other administrators, everyone dreamed about Carmel, about the miraculous rain of silver/money, falling from sacred heights in a religious glory" (5:169). The religious terminology of this passage is suggestive of the mentality of the smaller investors present at the meeting. The economic miracle by which money produces money gives rise to a faith as blind and boundless as any religious faith could be. Saccard has indeed founded a new Carmelite order whose members are awestruck before the profit-creating power of the Banque Universelle.

The symbolic significance of the Carmel silver mine is more extensive still. My analysis of *Au Bonheur des Dames* in the preceding chapter demonstrated how the expansion of Mouret's department store seemed to occur in ever-widening concentric circles until it reached outside France into foreign countries as well. *L'Argent* must be seen as a more decisive initiative in the same direction, namely, toward a form of imperialism. The projects to be financed by the Banque Universelle are presented in two different lights. Hamelin sees them as an attempt to civilize the Orient, to introduce a more rational (i.e., Western) order into a territory that is lying fallow: "Industry and commerce would increase tenfold, civilization would be victorious, and Europe would finally open its doors to the Orient" (5:63). However, the darker side of the economic invasion of the Orient implicit in Hamelin's remarks quickly becomes explicit: the so-called "civilizing" undertaking also amounts to a rapacious profit-grabbing enterprise. Saccard, untouched by Hamelin's religious fervor, expresses this view in rather bald terms: "It was for him as if speculation, the monetary economy, would swiftly conquer the old world, as if it were a new prey, still intact, of incalculable richness hidden beneath the ignorance and dirt of the centuries. He could almost smell the treasure, neighing like a war horse at the smell of battle" (5:75). The vocabulary leaves little doubt as to intentions. For Aristide, the point is not to civilize, but to exploit. Describing the attitude of capitalist adventurers such as Saccard, Hannah Arendt remarks tellingly, "The owners of superfluous capital were the first of the class [the bourgeoisie] to want profits without fulfilling some real social function."[4] The hallmark of Saccard's plans, the Carmel mine, vividly represents the attempt at a quick penetration into an economically underdeveloped region in order to extract high profits with no concern for the well-being of the indigenous population. Aristide and the hardened speculators of his inner group exploit the mine not so much as a real, material investment, but as a symbolic model that galvanizes and stimulates greed. It captures the essence of the imperialist drive toward exploitation for profit in areas that still lie outside the reaches of capitalist development.

The dynamics of speculation in Saccard's bank go far beyond the symbolic Carmel mine, however. The pursuit of profit within the Universelle centers much more fundamentally on the bank's stock shares, not simply on the dividends those shares pay, but rather on the *buying and selling* of the shares themselves. We would do well to consider the nature of those stock shares more carefully. At a first level, one could say that they are paper goods in much the same way as the deeds encountered in *La Curée*: they are signifiers that enter into circulation detached from any referent. But whereas a deed in the end always comes back to its referent, to the piece of property for which it stands, the referent in the case of a stock share is much more problematic. The holder is not interested in any material commodity but, rather, in participating in projected financial profits created by the company that has issued the stock. The share and its value are based upon the money generated by the company. In short, the stock share appears as a signifier of money itself, a signifier of the universal signifier.

The question of determining the worth of a stock share is therefore complex and delicate. It possesses first what may be termed a nominal worth. In the case of the Banque Universelle, for example, the price of each share is set at 500 francs. More interesting, however, is the fact that stock shares are exchangeable: they can be bought and sold. There is even a specialized market for such transactions, the stock exchange. The existence of such a market means that the nominal price of stock shares quickly becomes secondary to a price set by the laws of supply and demand characteristic of the market. Quite simply put, the greater the demand for a given stock, the higher the price. The signifier itself becomes a sort of commodity in its own right, one that possesses very peculiar characteristics. It is emptied of any conceivable use value, and its exchange value is itself exchangeable. In the stock market, the distance between the sphere of material reality and that of financial operations increases dramatically. This tendency is further radicalized by the fact that buying and selling operations are possible in which the speculator never actually takes delivery of the shares in question, never actually possesses them. In operations for future delivery, the only essential thing is a price differential which marks either a profit or a loss for the speculator. This type of operation requires only a minimum of funds deposited with a broker as a guarantee that the debt incurred by an unsuccessful operation will be covered. The hardened speculators in *L'Argent*—Sabatini, Baroness Sandorff, Bohain—do nothing but cash in price differentials and then often refuse to cover their losses when the difference is not in their favor.

The process whereby the signifier itself becomes a commodity finds illustration in *L'Argent* when a leitmotiv present in the two other financial novels we have studied is taken up once again and given a new development. In *L'Argent,* gold has left Saccard's fa-çade and Mouret's desk to reappear in the basement of Kolb's bank (Kolb being one of the inner group of speculators associated with Saccard's project). In a traditional context, the idea of placing gold in a basement (underground) would be equivalent to the act of hoarding, of constituting a treasure, a thesaurus, in the etymolog-ical sense. The context has changed, however, and in *L'Argent,* things are exactly the contrary. Gold appears in the basement not to interrupt circulation, but precisely to speed it up even further. Kolb's basement is, in reality, a foundry where the gold contained in coins is melted down into ingots to be sold as a commodity. Kolb is "a banker who specialized in arbitrages on gold, buying numerary in states where its market value was low, then melting it down in order to sell the ingots elsewhere, in countries where the price of gold was rising" (5:83). In the advanced financial sys-tem described in *L'Argent,* the universal signifier itself can become a commodity. If one wants to earn any appreciable profit by melt-ing down coins, speed and rapid turnover are of the utmost im-portance. "And, since morning, more than six million francs [of the metal] had gone through the process, bringing the banker a profit of barely three or four hundred francs. Arbitrage on gold, the differential occurring between two price quotations, was ex-tremely small, measured by thousandths, and yielded profits only on large quantities of the metal" (5:109). Gold, like securities, has become the object of "differences," of profits gained by min-imal fluctuations in price.[5] My focus on the leitmotiv of gold in the financial novels I have treated shows the central importance of the precious metal in revealing certain characteristics of the stages of speculation described in the three works. To grasp the signifi-cance of gold in its various incarnations is to reveal fundamental differences and continuities between the novels.

The motor of Saccard's enterprise, then, is the buying and sell-ing of stock shares in order to create profitable differences in their price. Let us now consider the effects of this new form of speculation on the problem of circulation that was central to the study of *La Curée* and *Au Bonheur des Dames*. The development of Saccard's own understanding of the process of circulation in *L'Argent* has noticeably matured since we left him in *La Curée*. Zola carefully places foils in Saccard's entourage who provoke explanations that reveal Aristide's new awareness. One such character is Caroline Hamelin, who continually objects to the speculation engendered by the Banque Universelle. The following remark is fairly typical of Aristide's responses to Caroline's misgivings and demonstrates that he has become as careful a theoretician of speculation as Octave was in *Au Bonheur*: "You must understand that speculation—risk—is the centerpiece, the very heart in a vast undertaking like ours. Yes! It pumps the blood, takes it everywhere from small streams, brings it together, sends it out in rivers in all directions, establishes an enormous circulation of money which is the very life of large business projects" (5:114–15). What was only implicit in *La Curée* has now become a veritable theory replete with a metaphorization establishing a parallel between the circulatory system and the economic system.[6] Speculation is calculated to increase the circulation of money by drawing it from the smallest of sources into the mainstream of economic life, combining many smaller amounts of capital into a more powerful whole.[7] In addition to increasing the amount of money in circulation, it increases the speed of circulation and combats economic stagnation. Saccard has occasion to explain this facet of the problem more clearly when he talks with the countess de Beauvilliers. The countess wishes to sell property that furnishes her yearly income in order to invest in the Banque Universelle. Saccard takes the opportunity to explain to her the functioning of the modern economic system:

> But, madam, no one earns a livelihood from the
> land anymore... The old estate has run its course as
> a form of wealth; it no longer has any reason to exist. It accomplished nothing but the stagnation of
> money, whereas we have increased its value tenfold
> by throwing it back into circulation as paper money
> and obligations of all sorts, both commercial and fi-

nancial. That's the way the world will be renewed,
because nothing was possible without money, liquid
cash which flows and penetrates everywhere.
(5:125–26)

The pertinent opposition here is between stagnation and flow, another incarnation of the opposition hardness/liquidity. Paper money, paper goods are the forms of wealth that provide for rapid circulation. The forum in which these signifiers may be bought and
sold, the stock exchange, creates profits in a realm as far removed
from any material referents as possible.

A fascinating counterpoint to the tendency away from the referent toward the signifier is provided in *L'Argent* by the figures of
Busch and his partner Mme Méchain. Busch is engaged in the
business of buying the rights to collect unpaid debts that creditors
have given up trying to collect themselves: "In addition to usury
and a whole hidden business in jewels and precious stones, he was
particularly involved in the purchase of bad debts" (5:33). What
he buys, in effect, are paper goods, those which are the furthest
removed from their sources: "And from these multiple sources,
paper goods would arrive, veritable basketfuls . . . unpaid bills,
unexecuted agreements, IOU's which had not been paid off, broken contracts" (5:34). He then uses these signifiers to retrace and
re-create the circumstances of their origin; in short, he moves from
the signifier to its referential source. Once he has identified that
source (the debtor), he awaits an opportunity to collect the outstanding debt: "As for debtors who had disappeared, they excited
him even more, launched him into a fever of continual research,
his eye on the announcements and names printed in the newpa-
pers, looking for addresses like a dog chasing his prey. As soon as
he laid his hands on those who had disappeared and were insolvent, he became ferocious, piled expenses on them, sucked them
dry" (5:34). Busch's activities follow a trajectory precisely opposite to that followed by Saccard and his fellow speculators. In a
sense, it could be said that he awaits them to bring them brutally
back to material realities should they make a false move in their
complicated maneuvers with their own paper goods. Saccard him-

self, as well as the countess de Beauvilliers, has occasion to experience the discomfort of being in Busch's grip.

If the price of stock shares results from the law of supply and demand, it behooves the speculator who directs the process not to leave the workings of that law to chance. Saccard plays the role of the bull in his stock speculations: he wishes to create a rise in the price of the Banque Universelle's stock shares in order to pocket the difference between the higher price and the original price. For there to be a constant rise in prices there must be a constant increase in the demand for Universelle shares. Consequently, Aristide must generate a dynamic process whereby more and more buyers become interested in the bank's stock. In an important sense, the narrative sequence of *L'Argent* is simply the story of a series of strategies aimed at achieving a regularly increasing demand for shares. As in *Au Bonheur des Dames,* chief among these strategies is a barrage of ever more striking advertisements. It became evident earlier that the Société des Mines d'Argent du Carmel was not particularly valuable in terms of the metal extracted from the mine, but rather because the project was "an excellent advertising operation," an idea that appealed to the desires of prospective investors. Aristide's strategy of inundating the city of Paris with favorable publicity during the organizational period of the Banque Universelle is next illustrated by his move to acquire a newspaper that he can control and use as a weapon. When Jantrou first proposes buying *L'Espérance,* Saccard is hesitant because of problems that might be caused by the political positions espoused by the newspaper. He is rapidly persuaded, however, that either a progovernment or an antigovernment stance has advantages. Furthermore, as the controlling interest in the paper, he will be at liberty to go one way or the other. The political question is quickly put aside in the interview with Jantrou when Saccard exposes his ultimate motive in acquiring the paper. " 'You will be the director,' " he tells Jantrou, " 'and I will take care of centralizing in your hands all of our advertising, which I want to be exceptional, enormous, especially later when we will be in a position to heat up the machine seriously' " (5:120).

The purchase of *L'Espérance* is but a first step in a process whereby increased excitement breeds ever-increasing publicity and vice versa. Saccard succeeds in building a positive feedback circuit that fuels his "machine," as he calls it. Working from their base in *L'Espérance*, Saccard and Jantrou purchase a number of smaller newspapers specializing in financial news. "Among the small financial papers which were multiplying profusely [Jantrou] had chosen and bought a dozen" (5:173). These smaller papers are already caught up in the swirl of publicity generated by financial institutions in search of investors:

> The best papers belonged to shady banks whose very
> simple tactic consisted in publishing them and giv-
> ing them away for a couple of francs per year. That
> sum did not even cover the price of postage, but
> they made up the loss in other ways by dealings us-
> ing the money and the stock shares of clients which
> the papers brought in. Under the pretext that they
> were publishing . . . all the technical information
> and figures which were useful to small investors,
> they then little by little began slipping in advertise-
> ments in the form of recommendations and advice,
> modest and reasonable at first, but soon without re-
> straint, with impudent tranquillity, bringing ruin
> to credulous subscribers. (5:173–74)

The trick, then, is to acquire those papers which have not yet abandoned the tone of honest advice and revealed their adventurous nature. Thus the coup for Saccard and Jantrou would be the acquisition of *La Côte financière*, "which already had twelve years of absolute probity behind it" (5:174). Meanwhile, *L'Espérance* conducts its own campaign in favor of the Banque Universelle, meticulously avoiding rhetorical excess: "Not a brutal campaign violently favorable, but rather explanations, discussions, a slow means of taking hold of the public and strangling it neatly" (ibid.). In addition to buying less important newspapers outright, Saccard and Jantrou set up a system of favors exchanged between *L'Espérance* and other Parisian publications. They do not hesitate, for example, to save shares in the Banque Universelle for those who adopt a favorable attitude toward their project. Nor do they disdain simply buying the silence of critical columnists. Through all of these maneuvers pierces "their immense disdain for the public, the scorn of the businessman's intelligence for the dark ignorance of the flock ready to believe any story . . . unschooled in the complicated transactions of the stock exchange" (5:176).

But publicity in itself is not functional if there is nothing of interest to publicize. The excitement initially provoked by the So- ciété des Mines d'Argent du Carmel must be extended by the appearance of further promising financial developments within the Universelle itself. Saccard discovers the perfect mechanism to spur the growth of the bank: periodic increases in capital assets. Within less than two years of existence, the bank twice doubles its capital, from 25 million francs to 50 million and finally to 100 million. In fact, a third increase in capital takes place just before the crash of January 1868. As the narrator says of this manipulation, "It was the classic combination, the way to spur on success, to make the price quotation gallop upwards with each new stock issue" (5:170). Combined with widespread publicity are operations calculated specifically to give the illusion of rapid and unlimited expansion. Whether increases in capital assets are justified or not, they are perfectly tailored to increase public confidence and thus to increase demand for Universelle shares. Their true nature is not substantive, reflecting the real financial development of the enterprise, but rather, formal, in that they create the appearance of such development. They can be considered as publicity stunts which complement and support the manipulation of information in newspapers.

The question of empty appearances brings us back to the problematic of the façade developed previously. If potential investors and depositors are to be impressed, the bank must allow these would-be customers to read the promise of success directly on the façade of its headquarters. As was the case with the solidification of Aristide's credit in *La Curée,* the beholder grants legitimacy to the speculative undertaking on the basis of what is visible to him. The process of formulating the Banque Universelle's image (to use a modern expression) falls into two phases. First, at the moment of foundation, emphasis must be placed on seriousness and solidity in order to inspire confidence in the Banque Universelle when it is but a newcomer to the financial world. The first location of the bank is in the princess d'Orviedo's residence. Saccard himself is "unhappy with the meanness of the locale" (5:138), limited in size by the constraints of available space. The final effect is quite striking, however, in its insistence upon certain reassuring characteristics:

> What was already striking when one entered, even
> in the midst of the crush caused by the construction
> workers who were driving in their last nails as the
> ring of gold coins could be heard from the depths of
> the cash boxes, was the air of severity, an air of an-
> cient probity vaguely suggestive of a sacristy. This
> atmosphere doubtless originated in the locale itself,
> the old dark and humid mansion, standing silently
> in the shade of the trees of the neighboring garden.
> One had the sensation one was penetrating into a re-
> ligious edifice. (5:139)

Using what is available within the chosen confines, the bank spontaneously adopts a religious register emblematic of the seriousness and honesty it wishes to exude in its early stages, thereby playing on the Catholic ideology that Saccard has taken over from Hamelin and reinserting itself into the network of religious imagery present from the start in the Carmel mine. Taking advantage of the circumstances to the fullest, Saccard then pushes things even further. He extends the façade from the realm of architecture into that of the very clothing and gestures used by the employees who people the architectural space: "Since one of his principles was always to use unexpected circumstances, he strained his ingenuity from then on in order to develop the austere appearance of the building. He demanded that his employees dress like young priests; everyone was required to speak in measured tones; money was received and paid out with clerical discretion" (ibid.).

Just as Saccard's modest beginnings in the domain of publicity with *L'Espérance* lead to the acquisition of more newspapers and the cultivation of a widening circle of allies in the press, so too the modest locale of the Universelle itself must necessarily give way to a more impressive installation as soon as the dynamic growth of the bank gains momentum. As always, Aristide dreams grand projects and wishes to make the second home of the bank truly monumental. Caroline objects to the luxury Saccard has planned, adopting the very argument he formulated originally: the new structure must favorably impress prospective investors. "Her avowed fear, her argument against all of this luxury was that the bank would lose its character of decent honesty, of deeply religious gravity" (5:229). However, Caroline's error consists in not seeing that at the moment when construction on the new bank building begins, in the fall of 1866, the growth of the bank has entered a new phase. Religious euphoria has given way to economic euphoria. The new atmosphere of adventure demands reinforcement from the Universelle in the form of an image that corresponds to public expectation. Aristide's argument favoring more luxurious quarters differs from Caroline's only in his perception of the public's present attitudes and desires: "Saccard, with the flair of a pickpocket, had felt the presence of this paroxysm on everyone's part, the need to throw money to the wind, to empty pockets and bodies. He had just doubled the funds destined to underwrite the advertising campaign" (5:231). What will clients used to the religious air of the original headquarters think of the new structure? "Saccard replied that they would be struck with admiration and respect, that those bringing in five francs would reach into their pockets and bring out ten, seized with pride, intoxicated with confidence" (5:229). Saccard's uncanny feel for public opinion leads him to another triumph and makes of the bank's new headquarters his most successful advertisement to date: "The success of the building was prodigious; the efficacy of the commotion it created surpassed even the most extraordinary advertisements conceived by Jantrou" (ibid.).

The link between the World's Fair and the Banque Universelle resurfaces characteristically in this context and provides the potential for an ironic counterpoint to the success of Saccard's project: the bank's new locale is so striking that it quickly attains the status of a semi-official exhibit: "And the various peoples with their

kings could come there and file by on the way to the fair" (ibid.).[8]
The bank becomes a monument to the empire's success—a success, however, that is already seriously undermined by hidden
weaknesses destined to appear rapidly in the form of bankruptcy
and military defeat. Napoleon III himself distributes prizes to the
exhibitors on the day of a bloody French debacle in Mexico: "That
very day news came to the Tuileries of the appalling catastrophe
in Mexico, the execution of Maximilian, French blood and gold
written off as a complete loss. The news was hidden in order to
avoid introducing a pall over the celebrations. It was the first death
knell at the end of this superb day sparkling in the sunlight"
(5:254). The luxury of the Banque Universelle's new headquarters
is so absolutely in step with public expectations that it turns out
to be eminently functional: it draws prospective clients and investors in droves. Saccard's taste for opulence is no longer idiosyn-
cratic, but is instead the very expression of the impulse of an entire
society. The catastrophic disaster about to befall him cannot in
this case be attributed to overinvestment in architectural artefacts,
but will instead be the result of wider and stronger forces that remain to be analyzed.

The importance of publicity in all its guises in *L'Argent* harks
back to the fundamental position of this mechanism in *Au Bonheur
des Dames*. Fashion was analyzed in that novel as a domain in which
the ravages of triangular desire were channeled into economics to
provide a dynamic impetus toward increasing turnover in circulation. The fashion retailer was seen as one who attempts to assume the position of a collective other, the third term (model) in
the triangle of desire, the one whose responsibility is to designate
what the customer must buy. In *L'Argent*, Saccard himself understands the power to be wielded by assuming the position of the
model through every possible publicity device. Stock-market
speculation is clearly another domain in which the structure of triangular desire is efficacious, perhaps even more so than in fashion.
Quite simply put, if the speculator buys stock shares with the hope
that their value will rise, he is in essence hoping that others will
think the same thing and will buy concurrently. Scrutinizing market trends ultimately means scrutinizing fellow buyers and doing

one's utmost to influence their decisions. The position of the other as model preexists in a very precise form in the realm of the stock market: it is the position of the pundit, the person whose successful operations give him an invincible air of expertise that others wish to emulate.

Saccard's seductive hold on prospective investors, who look to him to make decisions for them, is present throughout *L'Argent* and is emblematically illustrated by his relations with Baroness Sandorff. Despite her "sensual indifference, the secret scorn which she had for men" (5:122), she is invariably drawn toward Saccard in search of insider information and becomes so dependent upon him that she agrees not only to a sexual liaison, but is unable to abandon him in time to avoid the catastrophe of the Banque Universelle. Others, the large numbers of small investors such as Dejoie, come to view Saccard almost as a god in his infallibility. When Aristide permits Dejoie to become the first outside investor in the Banque Universelle, "Dejoie's face was radiant, as if he had just been blessed by an unexpected act of grace" (5:129). Whenever Dejoie doubts thereafter of the success of his investment, a simple look of confidence from Saccard will suffice to allay his fears. Saccard delivers so often on his promises that only the most cynical and hardened market players are able to escape his influence—and even then not always without difficulty. Daigremont is still staunchly supportive of Saccard when, on the eve of the decisive confrontation with Gundermann, he tells Baroness Sandorff not to sell her Universelle shares: "Tomorrow we'll be the masters" (5:322). Only a last-minute visit by Delarocque, bringing information on the strategy to be employed by Gundermann, allows Daigremont to avoid the crash and leaves him dismayed that he could have followed Saccard so blindly as far as he did: "Ah! What a lesson! This time he had almost let himself be toyed with like a child" (5:323). Such is the power of Saccard that only one broker and investor appears to be immune to it—Gundermann himself. However, the question of Gundermann's relative freedom in his confrontation with Saccard is problematic, as we shall see shortly.

Saccard's strategies for provoking the rise in value of Universelle shares have now been outlined. It has become evident that his bull position condemns him to a situation in which, as the narrator puts it, "every morning [must] bring a new rise in price, people [must] always believe in increasing success, monumental bank counters, enchanted counters which absorb streams in order to give back rivers, oceans of gold" (5:216). As the rise continues, ever-increasing means are required to fuel it: an expanding network of financial newspapers to carry the Universelle's name to more people, a headquarters worthy of the bank's pretensions to dominance, exaggerated augmentations of capital assets designed to suggest expanding and successful investments. While the market rise on Universelle shares pursues its course, those who are basing their activities upon it—Saccard and his allies—become ever more engaged in it. The slightest weakening in the position of the bank's shares would bring about the financial ruin of the bulls. Thus, although Saccard and company manipulate the market shamelessly, they do not do so with impunity, for they are themselves absolutely bound to it, at the mercy of the slightest slowdown, the slightest loss of confidence that could initiate a downward trend. A slowdown, moreover, would not be gradual and easy to parry, but would instead bring instant collapse. Upon seeing a downward slide develop, all the bulls, all those speculating on a rise, would immediately reverse their positions and become bears with the same solidarity, the same movement *en masse,* that characterized their original euphoria and confidence. The mechanism of the stock market tightens the bonds of mediated, triangular desire. I look at the other, and he looks at me. We must do precisely the same thing or one of us will lose. As soon as one important investor, one pundit, changes his position, a shock wave emanates out toward all the others, who necessarily follow suit. An inevitable feedback circuit is thus formed and constantly threatens to provoke an uncontrollable run.[9]

The results of Saccard's stock-market speculation, then, are quite paradoxical. On the one hand, the founding of the Banque Universelle and the subsequent playing in the stock market it engenders may be seen as a system in which the absence of the material commodity in any recognizable form permits increased circulation and therefore increased profits. On the other hand, the creation of a new type of "commodity," the stock share, while permitting quicker profits, also accentuates the dangers that accompany speculation. Once again it becomes possible to find oneself in the position of one who possesses too much of a given commodity, who has invested too heavily in a particular stock, and who finds himself unable to get rid of the suddenly unwanted commodity. The inability to sell the shares one owns does not simply interrupt circulation; it provokes catastrophic losses. Once the downward trend begins, panic can immediately set in and touch off a stampede of selling. In January 1868, the Universelle's shares are worth more than three thousand francs. Within a matter of days, the most one can get for them is a few francs from vultures like Busch and Mme Méchain. Saccard's new invention, market speculation, is extremely volatile. It is clearly superior to the speculative systems outlined in *La Curée* and *Au Bonheur des Dames* in its profit-making ability. However, the signifiers which the stock-market investor has succeeded in detaching from any referent must now stand *absolutely on their own*. If a collapse occurs, one is left literally with worthless pieces of paper. The push toward a new level of abstraction in economics is thus a mixed blessing—infinitely more powerful and yet infinitely more dangerous. It prompts Saccard to search for a final solution, an ultimate strategy that would give him an impregnable position. That strategy will be an attempt to corner the market.

Bull against Bear

Before turning to the final phase of Saccard's struggle to conquer the market—and Gundermann in the process—I would like to consider the implications of the thematic representation of speculation in the stock market as it is described in *L'Argent*. The maneuverings at the heart of Saccard's enterprise are often portrayed in the novel as irrational, euphoric, fantastic. The narrator characterizes the atmosphere well when he reveals Caroline's fear of Saccard's excesses: "She was far from being naïve, a simpleton one could fool. Even if she was ignorant of the technique involved in bank operations, she understood perfectly the reasons for the strain, the feverish activity aimed at intoxicating the crowd, at drawing it into the epidemic madness caused by the dance of millions" (5:216). The pertinent terms here are "intoxicating" (*griser*) and "madness" (*folie*), which emphasize a loss of control, an inability to act objectively, to think logically. *Griser* also contains the euphoric connotations of drunkenness. Furthermore, the occurrence of "epidemic" (*épidémique*) in the passage characterizes the quick-spreading repercussions of even the slightest reversals within a group bound as tightly by imitation as the group of speculators. Moreover, *épidémique* suggests the unsanitary atmosphere that, according to the narrator, both gives rise to and results from speculation, a thematic argument bolstered by the presence of the word "feverish" (*enfièvrement*). More than once the Banque Universelle and institutions like it are described as mushrooms having sprung up on the unsavory terrain of the Second Empire: "The proliferation of shady enterprises, overheated by advertisement, which had grown like monstrous mushrooms in the decomposed compost of the regime" (5:315).

Not only do such passages explicitly link the economic practices at stake with the political regime in which they are encouraged, but they amount to rather outright condemnations of stock speculation. The question of the ideological position adopted concerning speculation in the novel is not quite so clear-cut, however. For every passage like those quoted in the preceding paragraph the reader can easily find a counterexample. One of Aristide's conversations with Caroline Hamelin comes immediately to mind:

> In fact, without speculation we couldn't do any
> business, my dear. . . . With the legitimate and
> mediocre remuneration for work, the prudent equi-
> librium of daily transactions, existence is a desert of
> extreme platitude, a swamp in which all the forces
> are asleep and stagnant. While on the other hand, if
> you make a dream flame violently on the horizon, or
> promise that with one penny people can earn a
> hundred, or offer a chance to all the people who are
> asleep to begin a hunt for the impossible, for mil-
> lions conquered in two hours in the midst of the

most appalling dangers, only then does the race begin. Energy increases tenfold, the crush is such that
while sweating solely for their pleasure, people
sometimes succeed in making children, I mean living things, great and beautiful... Ah, yes, there is
much useless filth, but the world would certainly
end without it. (5:136)

This impassioned defense of speculation is simultaneously a locus
of fundamental ambivalence. Aristide champions unbridled desire
because it seems to be the only way to release energies that can
lead to constructive development of the economy. In his terms,
illegitimate children are a necessary evil occurring in the process
of producing legitimate ones—a certain amount of "useless filth"
is inevitable. The dilemma of means and ends will not be solved
in any unambiguous fashion in the text. Even in his spectacular
failure, which brings the ruin of countless others, Saccard will re-
tain some of his heroic aura, as the final interview between him
and Caroline reveals: "And despite herself, out of her terror, a certain admiration arose. Abruptly, in this miserable, bare prison cell,
locked tight, cut off from living beings, she had just felt a sensation of exuberant force, . . . the eternal illusion of hope, the stub-
bornness of a man who does not want to die" (5:387). Zola's text
systematically undermines and neutralizes ideological stances that
threaten to simplify complex moral questions and to reduce polysemy to a single possible interpretation, as Philip Hamon has
convincingly demonstrated: "*Mixture* and *dissociations* of morally
antagonistic universes [are] doubtless the solutions which the author will employ with the greatest predilection in order to 'neu-
tralize' an evaluative system which is too discriminating, too fo-
calizing."[10]

The condemnation of speculation has been evident elsewhere in
the *Rougon-Macquart*. We saw how speculation was linked to incest
in *La Curée* and how it implied the exploitation of women in *Au
Bonheur des Dames*. In a very real sense, before *L'Argent,* speculation
has a decidedly parasitic air about it. Despite all arguments to the
contrary in *La Curée*—the creation of jobs resulting from Haussmann's renovation projects, for example—the fact remains that

those who really profit from such projects are the speculators whose buying and selling artificially raises prices. Ultimately, the government pays exorbitant sums of money for an unproductive movement of fictitious deeds. Through government indemnities, the speculators obtain money collected from actively productive citizens and thus may be viewed as parasites who live off the pro-
ductivity of other sectors of the economy. Moreover, Mouret's aim in *Au Bonheur* is to create a secondary system of commodities not essential to existence in order to entrap precisely those who have been forced to live their lives cut off from production—women.

The parasitic structure of speculation is mirrored clearly in the mode of Napoleon III's political power. The emperor's position within the Second Empire is also parasitic. Far from representing any political group, he instead preys upon all classes equally. Marx condemns this new form of political exploitation precisely as a "frightful parasitic body, which surrounds the body of French society like a caul and stops up all all its pores."[11] The same exploitation is reproduced in the relationship between the emperor and his own supporters. As a younger member of the legislature remarks in a scene of *Son Excellence Eugène Rougon*, "[Napoleon III's] coffers are being pillaged. . . . He only allowed himself to be named emperor so that he could enrich his friends. . . . This is money which is being given back to France" (2:173). A rather ironic comment, to be sure, for it is obvious that the money gets back only to a selected few allies. Marx sums up derisively: "The financial science of the lumpenproletariat, of both the genteel and the common variety, is restricted to gifts and loans. These were the only springs Bonaparte knew how to set into motion."[12]

In a fundamental sense, the speculator is viewed as a prestidigitator, one skilled in making something out of nothing, one who has turned away from the solid reality of the referent toward the artificial construction of a world of simulacra. This basic difference between the old and the new economy is emblematically represented in a novel that ostensibly has little to do with questions of economics, *L'Oeuvre*. However, *L'Oeuvre* is a work treating the confrontation between old and new not only in the artistic domain, but also in the marketplace. That confrontation is illustrated by the differences between the two art dealers in the novel, Malgras and Naudet. Malgras's visit to Claude Lantier's studio in the second chapter is an obvious attempt to profit from Claude's contempt for material questions in order to obtain his best works at the cheapest possible price. Nonetheless, the narrator evinces a begrudging respect for Malgras, which, by implication, is shared by Sandoz, Dubuche, and Claude. Despite outward appearances, Malgras "was a very astute fellow who had a taste and a flair for good painting. He was never sidetracked by mediocre daubers. By instinct he went straight to the personal artists, to those whose talents were still disputed and for whom his flaming red drunkard's nose smelled a great future in the distance" (4:54). The important point here is that Malgras has the taste, the flair, the intelligence, to recognize truly good painting. His instinct seems quite infallible, and he is interested in nothing but the best. Moreover, although he drives a hard bargain, he has retained the characteristics of the traditional merchant in his dealings. He never buys without already having a customer for his merchandise, and he limits his own profits to a respectable minimum: "He was content with a decent profit, twenty percent, thirty percent at most, having based his business on the rapid renewal of his small capital investment, never buying in the morning without knowing to which of his collectors he would sell that evening" (ibid.). Even Malgras's customers share in his appreciation of true artistic talent: they are themselves "amateurs." In the absence of *real* art, Malgras would not be engaged in the business of being a dealer.

Naudet is an entirely different story, diametrically opposed to Malgras, as the text of the novel makes explicit:

> He was a dealer who, for several years now, had been
> revolutionizing the selling of paintings. With him,
> it was no longer a question of the old style, of the
> dirty frock coat and the astute taste of old Malgras,
> of lying in wait for beginners' paintings, buying
> them for ten francs, and reselling them for fifteen—
> in short, of the nickel-and-dime game of the con-
> noisseur. . . . No, the famous Naudet had the style
> of a gentleman . . . [and] lived expensively. . . .

Ultimately, he was a speculator, a stock-market
dealer who didn't give a whit about good painting.
He possessed a unique flair for success, he knew how
to choose the right artist to launch—not the one
who had the promise of the controversial genius belonging to the great painter, but the one whose dishonest talent, overblown with false daring, was
going to make money in the bourgeois market.
Thus he succeeded in changing that market drasti-
cally, by removing the previously important con-
noisseurs, who bought for their taste, and by doing
business only with the rich collectors, who knew
nothing about art and bought a painting as they
would a stock share, out of vanity and in the hope
that its price would go up. (4:185–86)

We are no longer concerned here with real talent, with works of
art destined to endure. Naudet's gaze is turned not toward the
artist, but toward the public. His instinct identifies consumer
trends in their incipient stages and capitalizes on them by publi-
cizing and launching artists to fulfill the public's desires. The talent of such artists is necessarily "dishonest," "overblown with false
daring," because it is geared to sell and not to create. The art objects at stake are false and empty, far removed from those which
attracted Malgras. Naudet succeeds because he addresses a new
public—not the connoisseur, but the new moneyed rich who are
absolutely bereft of esthetic judgment and who buy paintings not
to appreciate them, but in hopes that their value, both cultural
and material, will rise like that of a stock share (i.e., will "appreciate"). Naudet and the new public are made for each other; he is
a speculator's speculator. For them the value of art objects no longer exists intrinsically, but is the creation of a market driven by
hype and by the same type of mediated, triangular desire so successfully employed by Mouret and Saccard. It is only fitting that
Naudet turns out to be the strongest backer of Fagerolles, the be-
trayer of Claude's ideals, who succeeds because he adjusts his artistic recipes to remain in step with public expectations.

Yet even the condemnation of Fagerolles and Naudet is fraught with ambivalence, given Claude's utter failure and his slide into madness and suicide. The one artist who supposedly possesses a profound talent experiences public and personal humiliation and catastrophe. Decidedly, the question of whether or not speculation is a positive activity is a complex one—for economists writing about the stock market in France around the time of the publication of *L'Argent* as well as for Zola himself. "The stock share—and the steam engine of which it facilitated the generalized development—are the two principal instruments of the great economic and social evolution which has been occurring in the last half century" and have "contributed to the development of the general well-being," says Edmond Théry.[13] While praising speculation, however, Théry is inevitably drawn to the financial scandals provoked by speculative practices and, in particular, to the crash of the Union Générale upon which *L'Argent* draws so heavily.[14] "Speculation in Lyon had surpassed all the madness of the Rue Quincampoix during the Regency. The rapid rise in the value of Union Généralé shares having quickly enriched certain businessmen in the city, . . . a gambling fever abruptly invaded all classes of the population."[15] Using a vocabulary akin to that used by Zola, Théry focuses upon the extremes to which speculation unfailingly leads. What begins as a development contributing to the "general well-being" always seems to end in a mad scramble for easy profit. Is a middle ground possible?

Another contemporary of Zola, Claudio Jannet, undertook a study of capital and speculation precisely in the hope of separating the good from the bad, the productive from the fraudulent, thereby establishing the middle ground upon which useful speculative ventures could take place. His initial premise resembles Théry's—or Saccard's, for that matter: "On the day the share or the security was invented, a veritable economic revolution took place."[16] However, although speculation is "legitimate and necessary," it also "leaves open the possibility of suspicious developments, fraudulent maneuvers" (Jannet, *Le Capital au XIXe siècle*, p. v). Legislation must be passed to punish those who abuse the manipulative potential of the stock exchange and related economic practices. But how does one distinguish the legitimate from the illegitimate?

Jannet bases his demarcation on the opposition between what is *real,* on the one hand, and what is *artificial, fictitious,* or attributable to *chance,* on the other: *"Gambling,* which is rightly condemned from the moral point of view, . . . is precisely the inverse of speculation. Instead of attempting to make a profit by evaluating the consequences of *real events* in the market, the gambler seeks a gain exclusively through *chance"* (*Le Capital au XIXe siècle,* p. 234; my emphasis). Chance, however, is the domain only of uninitiated speculators. Those who possess the means to speculate on a large scale always have recourse to artificial measures in order to gain some effective control over stock-market prices—shortages provoked by secretly stockpiling certain shares, unwarranted increases in the capital reserves of companies they control, distribution of fictitious dividends which reflect no actual profit but serve solely to increase the demand for stock shares.

As could be expected, it is difficult for Jannet to define clearly what he means by "real" facts or conditions. At times the term seems to suggest what is reasonable and normal, at other times, what is tangible in a company's assets. The opposition real/fictitious, however, immediately encounters a most troublesome case. A good deal of market speculation is based on operations for future delivery. The speculator agrees to buy or sell at a future date stock shares (or commodities) he does not presently possess. Such operations would seem destined to fall into the class of the fictitious, since they take place wholly at the level of price differentials and concern no tangible, real object. Not so, claims Jannet:

> In futures operations, the seller must deliver the
> merchandise on a specific date. If he does not actual-
> ly possess it, the sale is termed a short sale [*à décou-
> vert*]. It has sometimes been said, as a result of a bad
> scholastic argument, that these contracts are not le-
> gitimate because they concern future things which
> do not exist in nature. This argument is false, be-
> cause the parties involved have come to terms not
> with respect to actual objects [*corps certains*], to ob-
> jects determined in their indivuality, but with re-

spect to fungible things. There is an absolute moral
certainty that the seller can procure these objects. It
is only a question of the price. (*Le Capital au XIXe
siècle*, p. 241)

The difficulty is manifest in Jannet's attempted analysis. What is
real does not necessarily have to be an "actual object" or an "object
determined in its individuality," but can also be a "fungible thing," ₁₅₁
which, according to Jannet, belongs to the realm of reality just as
much, if not in quite the same way, as any "actual object." The
distinctions, needless to say, are less than convincing. The fact
that speculation is possible in the absence of the "thing" means
that any third party outside the "normal" circuit of exchange between producer and consumer can intercept a transaction and turn
it to his own profit. Such third parties are termed parasites by Jannet at one point: "Indeed, people who engage in commercial speculations without being wholesalers or retailers, without truly being
involved in the business, are not only guilty of a serious imprud-
ence, but are parasites" (ibid., p. 279). As a third party who inserts himself into a circuit that "normally" should exclude him,
the speculator occupies a position structurally comparable to that
of Napoleon III in the political arena.

In his attempt to illustrate the triumph of "reality" over "fiction," Jannet ultimately conceives of a statistical definition of the
real, thereby apparently avoiding the vexing problem of deciding
with precision to which category specific financial operations belong. Modern means of communication and dissemination of information added to global financial strategies have eliminated to
some extent the local fluctuations that used to bring quick fortunes to small-time speculators and have thus introduced increased regularity into financial transactions. "Thanks to constant
and regular information, the large-scale speculations that occur
today are always directed, not against the reality of the facts, but
toward their confirmation" (*Le Capital au XIXe siècle*, p. 243).
Reality would thus be the overall market tendencies that prevail
despite momentary disturbances. According to this conception,
the source of sanity would lie in global statistics, upon which suc-

cessful traders must rely. The distant and impersonal basis that large numbers seem to provide soon exhibits important flaws, however. In particular, statistics are produced by the very parties who attempt to use them, and consequently, they cannot be the ultimate bastion of objectivity one may wish them to be: "Today people have recourse to false statistics concerning production in order to influence stock prices" (ibid., p. 280)

Try as one might, eliminating the potential for manipulation is nothing short of an impossibility. The crux of the matter is that speculative transactions are both beneficial and potentially harmful. Moreover, in all but the most obvious cases, it is not possible to distinguish with great clarity between the good and the bad aspects of speculation. Having begun in the hope of establishing a set of clear distinctions, Jannet concludes that such an attempt must fail: "One must . . . come to the conclusion that no law can sanction these abuses, because no legal definition can distinguish the legitimate and serious transactions from the fictive and fraudulent ones" (ibid., p. 283). The ambivalence toward speculation that haunts Zola's text is thus far from being an isolated phenomenon and appears instead to inhabit contemporary analyses of the subject.

As was suggested earlier by means of a comparison between Saccard and Jadwin of Frank Norris's *The Pit,* French and American attitudes toward speculative practices at the end of the nineteenth century contained some close parallels. In an analysis of Dreiser's *The Financier* related to the present study, Walter Benn Michaels has revealed the premises at work in the activities of another celebrated fictional manipulator, Frank Cowperwood—premises which by now have a familiar ring.[17] The evolution of Cowperwood's career is characteristic in light of our analysis of speculation. He begins as a commodities broker. The exchange of tangible goods offers a certain stability, a means of earning a steady and relatively assured gain. But it puts material limits on circulation (how much can be sold and how fast) and thus on the profit one can expect. Commodities begin to bore Cowperwood, who soon realizes that there is more money to be made in what Michaels terms the "abstraction" of financial operations. The trick is precisely to begin dealing in prices and money, not in wheat or corn (nor, as in the case of Saccard's early career, in real estate). Although the market fluctuations which permit speculation can be dangerous, the stakes are considerably higher. Moreover, if one turns market fluctuations into a sort of abstract commodity, one can hope to harness them to some extent and thereby to increase profits enormously: "Cowperwood . . . not only takes advantage of these fluctuations, he goes one step further; he creates them— they *are* his commodities, the source of his profit" (Michaels, "Dreiser's *Financier,*" p. 280). The true speculator is not at the mercy of rising or falling prices, but is instead the very *source* of those movements.

The conceptual conflict in *The Financier* between the tangible and the abstract reproduces in slightly altered terms Jannet's distinction between the real and the artificial. And once again, the distinction turns out to be much less clear than it first appears. It is not easy to decide, for example, whether, as Michaels puts it, "value is a function of production or of speculation" (ibid., p. 281). Is the source of profit in exchange operations to be found in the tangible work accomplished originally by the producer of commodities, or, on the contrary, is profit the result of the abstract nature of the very exchange process itself? The interesting fact is that within the American context of this debate, a very familiar test case appears immediately—the problem of futures operations. In the eyes of American economists, futures contracts were theoretically justified as a means of protecting both seller and buyer from any sudden radical fluctuations in price. They were a mechanism designed to permit smoother large-scale commodity sales in an economy that was growing too complex for traditional direct exchange. "In practice, however, the futures market, in the eyes of producers and consumers both, seemed mainly to provide a source of profit for a whole new class of middlemen who neither produced nor consumed commodities but speculated in them" (ibid.). Attempts made to distinguish between legitimate and illegitimate futures contracts by certain American agrarian interests met with a failure quite akin to Claudio Jannet's. The difficulty encountered was that "of distinguishing between hedging (as a form

of insurance), legitimate speculating, and outright gambling"
(ibid., p. 282). On the surface, market operations are all mechan-
ically the same. It is only at the level of intentions that differences
appear, but intentions can be interpreted only subjectively: "The
distinction in fact rests essentially on a question of intention, not
even on the part of both parties involved, but often with reference

to only one of them" (Jannet, *Le Capital au XIXe siècle*, p. 283).
Like French econo.nic analysts, Americans saw the necessity and
utility of speculation but were troubled by its deep-rooted tendency to overrun productive economic activity and ultimately to
devalue it. The resulting situation was morally and economically
dangerous—for all but the rare genius at financial affairs, that is.

This ambivalence is embodied in the two financial geniuses who
run afoul of each other in *L'Argent*. The struggle between Saccard
and Gundermann is a confrontation of two speculators who each
seek to master the dangerous mechanisms of financial manipulations. As in *La Curée*, the Saccard of *L'Argent* is presented as a poet
driven more by dreams and ardent desires than by logic and reason. "With sweeping generalizations in his ardent language, he
would transform a business transaction into a poetic story" (5:101).
Having encountered and known defeat, he has nonetheless refused
to temper his flights of fancy, to abandon his impassioned manner
for a calmer, more careful approach to financial affairs: "In truth,
he was attaining a certain grandeur, with his gestures reaching up
to the stars, like a poet of money who had become no more prudent
despite bankruptcies and ruin" (5:243). The illogical and fanciful
nature of Saccard's passion is partially illustrated by the thematics
of chance developed by the narrator. Aristide is a "fatalist believing in chance" (5:102), and thus, despite all his maneuvering, there
are certain limits to his action. Once he sets a plan into motion,
for example, he is loath to alter it. In such circumstances, "he
[demonstrates] the ferocity of the gambler who does not want to
change his luck" (5:196). Chance and luck do indeed play an essential part in Saccard's early success with the Banque Universelle:
he has the good fortune to learn before anyone else of a telegram
announcing a peace treaty that permits him to make a quick kill-
ing in the market and to improve his bank's financial position in

one blow. "Therein lay one of those chains of circumstances which make up lucky breaks . . . removed from all reason and logic" (5:198). In fact, the telegram episode is what ultimately establishes Saccard's reputation as a pundit. Luck therefore passes for knowledge, as is habitually the case in the stock market.

By bestowing an irrational, illogical character upon the speculation that develops in *L'Argent,* the narrative permits the subsequent strategy of playing such speculation off against what is considered a more logical norm of behavior. Ultimately, the question of the logical and of how Saccard's speculative undertaking defies the logical is fundamental to the novel. The spokesman for logic is Gundermann, and his theory is quite simple. As the narrator explains it, "Logic alone reigned supreme. In questions of speculation, as elsewhere, truth was an all-powerful force. As soon as prices became too exaggerated, they would collapse: the decline would then occur mathematically" (5:202). Elsewhere the Jewish financier completes his theory in more detail: "There is thus a maximum value which [a stock share] must not reasonably exceed. And as soon as it does exceed that value as a result of the public's infatuation, the increase is factitious. Wisdom then lies in positioning oneself for a fall in price with the certainty that it will occur" (5:265). "Logic," "truth," "mathematically," "reasonably," "wisdom," "certainty": these are the terms that characterize the theory challenging Saccard in the marketplace.

Not only is Gundermann the spokesman for logic opposed to Saccard the irrational dreamer, he is the embodiment of that logic. The description of Gundermann furnished by the narrator leaves little room for doubt: "This figure, no longer of the classic miser who hoards, but of the impeccable worker, without fleshly needs, who had become almost abstract in his suffering old age" (5:96). Contrary to Saccard, Gundermann is "without fleshly needs," a mere abstraction, emptied of the ferocious desires that drive Saccard. The Jewish financier's response to Saccard's offer to include him in the Banque Universelle's founding group is characteristic. Despite the fact that Saccard correctly senses the austere atmosphere of Gundermann's existence and is therefore reserved in his description of the Banque Universelle, he elicits only a negative response from the financier: "You'll fall—and heavily—without fail, it's mathematical, because you are too impassioned, you have too much imagination" (5:97). The opposition between the two businessmen is carried even further. Saccard is a "speculator, a captain of adventures, maneuvering others' millions" (5:94). Gundermann, on the other hand, is a "simple money merchant" (5:95), one who possesses a personal fortune with which to maneuver, one who therefore needs no one else: "One's own million thus maneuvered is an impregnable force" (ibid.).

The opposition Saccard/Gundermann seems straightforward enough at first glance. But its very simplicity obscures a fundamental problem which will become a focal point as the novel advances: the difficulty in discerning the difference between the logical and the illogical, the normal and the excessive, in matters concerning speculation on the stock exchange. Such oppositions echo at yet another level those we have already noted in the works of French and American economic theorists of the period. Gundermann and the narrator act as if it were a simple mathematical task to determine what could be considered the logical, normal price of any given stock share, when in fact, such a calculation is much more difficult than the reader is led to believe, if not simply impossible. As Jean Bouvier writes with reference to the crash of the Union Générale in 1882 (an event that provided a model for much of L'Argent),

> The term "excess," readily used in the financial press
> of the period [1881], is furthermore quite incorrect,
> since it suggests that one could define a "normal"
> field of bank and stock-market activities beyond
> which the practitioners would become prone to ad-
> venture and economic error. The law of profit, the
> scramble for earnings, the competitive struggle, so-
> cial emulation: when applied to stock markets, these
> forces ultimately render illusory and impossible any
> definition of this sort. [18]

Bouvier suggests that stock-market speculation is a domain of competition for profit wherein a tendency toward maximization with little respect for any so-called limits of normality is inherent. Consequently, a distinction between two apparently opposing speculators in *L'Argent* based on the concept of the logical is faulty, and it ultimately masks more fundamental phenomena.

Try as he might to remain a cold rationalist evincing his disdain for the stock market by never setting foot in the edifice that houses it, Gundermann is much more a slave to it than he would admit: "In order to establish the foundations of his power, he needed to dominate the stock market. Thus, on each settling day there was a new battle in which victory was infallibly his through the decisive virtue of his overwhelming force" (5:95). In Saccard, who has rapidly succeeded in becoming a formidable power in the Parisian stock market, Gundermann has encountered a dangerous rival. That rival is all the more threatening because he has begun proving that the maxims concerning normality and excess in the market are not really applicable. "In his convictions, in his absolute belief in logic, [Gundermann] nonetheless remained surprised by Saccard's rapid conquests, by this force which had suddenly sprung up and which was beginning to frighten the big Jewish banks" (5:265). If he is to preserve his supremacy in the market, Gundermann must at all costs counter Saccard. Thus, when he begins to assume the bear's role (i.e., playing for a fall in Universelle prices), he does so not because of the excesses of a rising market, but because he hopes that his weight can halt the rise and inflict a resounding defeat on Saccard. In short, the financier's strategy is as much one of self-preservation and self-interest as of good sense, and the rhetoric concerning the maximum logical value of given stock shares appears a mere rationalization rather than a convincing argument: "He needed to demolish this dangerous rival as soon as possible . . . in order not to have to share his royalty in the market with that terrible adventurer, whose death-defying stunts seemed to succeed against all good sense, as if by miracle" (5:265–66).

How does Gundermann combat Saccard? Although he adopts a market position diametrically opposed to that of Saccard (bear instead of bull) in order to beat Saccard, in reality, *he becomes more and more like him*—despite the narrator's attempts to maintain the distinction between the two men: "Gundermann, full of contempt for passion, exaggerated even further the impassivity of his mathematical gamble, with the cold obstinacy of a man of numbers, always selling despite the continued rise, losing greater sums on each settling day, with the unshakable assurance of the prudent man who simply deposits his money in his savings account" (5:266). It would be difficult not to read ironically the narrator's comment that the financier is "full of contempt for passion." On the contrary, Gundermann becomes passionately involved in his battle against Saccard, to the point of exaggerating the characteristics of his own personality—the "impassivity of his mathematical gamble," for example—in a manner that seems no less irrational than Saccard's behavior. Speculating for a fall despite colossal losses, he becomes caught in the same vicious circle as Saccard. Unbeknownst even to himself, Gundermann has begun to act according to a different kind of logic, that of unmitigated speculation. From the beginning, Saccard has wholeheartedly assumed the adventurous and risky side of his speculative undertaking. Now, for the first time, Gundermann glimpses the possibility of defeat and in turn throws himself into a machine which seems as out of control as the locomotive roaring through the night at the end of *La Bête humaine*. The opposition between norm and excess that is a leitmotiv of *L'Argent* is subverted once this final battle is fully engaged. I would maintain that it is Saccard's logic which has subsumed the original opposition, not Gundermann's.

That logic is indeed as powerful and as mathematically sound as anything Gundermann has opposed to it. Consider the mechanism of speculating for a fall in price in a futures operation. As Gaston Défossé explains succinctly, "The principal party hopes, in fact, that between the date when he sells and the settling date, the value of the share will fall so that he can buy it back in order to make good on his previous sale and thus realize a profit."[19] Ideally, the seller can sell at one price shares he actually does not possess and later buy shares of the same stock at a lower price in order to be able to deliver the shares he has sold on the date of maturity. The difference in the two prices is his profit. But what happens if the price rises instead of falling? If the seller "has sold short [i.e., without actually possessing any shares of the stock], he can even encounter grave difficulties in finding shares to make good on his sales contract. The price thus rises in a continual fashion, driven by the short-sellers, who are trying to buy to cover themselves and who succeed only at a very high price. They are said to be *squeezed* [*étranglés*]."[20] As long as a rise in prices persists, those who adopt a bearish position by means of futures operations actually further fuel the rise. The bears dealing in Banque Universelle shares in *L'Argent* encounter difficulties not only in continually paying off their losses but finally even in finding the shares that must be delivered at the maturity of their futures contracts. "Most certainly many were selling short and were forced to carry over their operations to the next settling day, because they were unable to deliver the shares" (5:313). In the end only Gundermann and his allies are able to absorb the losses incurred and still sustain the campaign against Saccard: "It was an invincible force to be able to continue selling short with the certainty that losses could always be paid off" (ibid.). This certainty, however, is predicated on Gundermann's ability to procure the shares he needs to sell at the maturity date of his futures operations. He is vulnerable to one strategy only—a corner on the market which would totally negate the possibility of obtaining those shares.

With this in mind, we must turn to Saccard's reaction in the face of Gundermann's concerted effort to end the rise in the Universelle's shares. As the Jewish financier's group begins speculating for a fall in prices and therefore selling Universelle shares short in large volume, Saccard encounters the problem of an oversupply of shares on the market. No amount of advertising or generated euphoria will be sufficient to absorb the sudden influx of Universelle stock, and as a result of the oversupply, the law of supply and demand threatens to provoke a fall in the price of shares. The solution is what might be termed the ultimate strategy: Saccard begins buying up his own bank's stock. Only in this way can he limit supply and sustain the rise.

Saccard's plan in the face of Gundermann's threat merits close scrutiny. Perhaps more than anything else he undertakes in the novel, it participates in all the ambiguity that obtains in the opposition between logical and illogical in the stock market. The practice of buying his own shares is not forced upon Saccard solely by the bears who attack him. From the founding moment of the Banque Universelle, he engages in the practice of keeping shares of its stock off the market. Caroline is the first to call attention to these questionable purchases: "I thought the law required that the full stock offering be sold." Aristide maintains in response that every young company does the same thing and says simply, "I prefer . . . to reserve some shares for us" (5:113), without further explanation. Only later, on the occasion of the second doubling of the bank's capital assets, does the problem arise again. Hamelin broaches the subject this time: "It makes me tremble to see that we are keeping such a large number of our shares. Not only do we not have that cash available, we are immobilizing ourselves; we shall end up devouring ourselves one day" (5:243–44). The objection is no longer simply legal; it has now become economic as well. Money tied up in the purchase of shares is money that cannot be used elsewhere, that is removed from circulation. The more money immobilized in this fashion, the less remains available to be employed profitably in other areas and the more tightly the bank is bound to the strategy of buying more of its shares in order to establish a "floor" for the prices of its stock. Being now a major holder of its own shares, it would be among the hardest hit by any decline in their value. Saccard's response clearly outlines his goals:

> "But we're not gambling!" cried Saccard. "However, it is permitted for us to bolster our stock, and we would really be inept if we weren't careful to prevent Gundermann and the others from devaluing our shares by playing against us for a fall. If they haven't yet dared to do much, that doesn't mean that they won't. That's why I'm rather satisfied to have a certain number of our shares in hand, and, I warn you, if I'm forced to, I'm ready to buy even more. Yes! I'll buy more rather than let the price fall one cent!"
> He had spoken those final words in an extraordi-

narily forceful tone, as if he had sworn to die rather
than to be beaten. (5:244)

The mixture of logical argument and much less logical passion is
striking in this passage. It is one thing to maneuver here and there
against an attack by Gundermann and his allies, but quite another
to decide from the very beginning, as Saccard has clearly done,
that the price of the shares should never be allowed to decline under any circumstances. The strategy of indiscriminate buying on
Saccard's part in order to fulfill what seems more and more to be
a dream ("I want to attain the price of three thousand francs") is
extremely disquieting to Caroline, who can only respond, "That's
crazy!" (ibid.). In the beginning, then, Saccard is pursuing an artificial goal by buying his own stock and is not competing directly
against Gundermann: "Three thousand francs: I want it, I'll get
it!" (5:246).

Hamelin's objections serve as a cue for the narrator himself, who
condemns in no uncertain terms the practice of a company's buying shares of its own stock: "Any company which wants to be master of the stock exchange in order to maintain the value of its own
stock is lost" (5:314). Nothing, however, prevents Saccard from
pursuing this course of action. Though he moderates his purchases
in the beginning, his enthusiasm and imagination get the better
of him, or so the narrator would once again have the reader believe. Soon he is irreparably engaged in buying up Universelle
shares: "However, even if his troops were winning big, Saccard
was at the end of his cash reserves, emptying his coffers for his
continual purchases" (ibid.). Yet as he advances in a seemingly
excessive direction, he begins to sense the real possibilities available to him: "He began dreaming extravagant dreams of conquest,
a mad idea so enormous that he couldn't even formulate it clearly
for himself" (ibid.). Try as the narrator might to characterize Saccard once more as extravagant and irrational, the fact is that by
pushing his strategy to the limit, Aristide actually discovers a superior logic that justifies his extremes. Despite his increasingly
precarious situation, an ultimate solution finally dawns upon him:

"And, already emptied of resources, reduced to using credit instruments, he now dared—like the starving who see immense feasts in the midst of their delirious hunger—to acknowledge to himself the prodigious and impossible goal toward which he was striving, the giant idea of buying back all the shares in order to have the short-sellers bound hand and foot at his mercy" (5:316). The opposition between logical and illogical is destined to be subsumed under a more powerful logic: to defeat Gundermann, Saccard must in effect squeeze out those who are speculating for a decrease in the value of Universelle shares. Such a squeeze is possible only if Saccard can corner the market. The stock shares/signifiers have concentrated financial resources to such an extent that to possess all of them would be tantamount to ending the struggle and obtaining a position of absolute mastery. The reader familiar with Norris's *The Pit* will recall that Jadwin also hits upon a corner on the wheat market as the means of defeating all his opponents.

Ultimately, Saccard does not succeed, but it should be clear by now that this is not the result of faulty reasoning on his part. The final position of mastery in the domain of stock speculation can only be a corner on the market. Despite the narrator's apparent condemnation of Aristide's attempt to create such a situation, that attempt comes tantalizingly close to success. Daigremont fails to lend his support at the precise moment of greatest necessity, which is, not surprisingly, also the moment when Saccard is closest to success. Nothing in the narrative precludes formally the possibility of success, despite the continued efforts by the narrator to present Saccard's goal as dreamlike or unreal.

The disaster that ensues from Aristide's failure is of a gravity equal to the greatness of his aspirations. Gundermann does triumph, but only by default and only by playing Saccard's game to the hilt. The opposition established between the two adversaries in the novel is far from remaining static. It is instead a locus of transformation toward a paradoxical resemblance as both speculators are drawn into the mimetic maelstrom of the stock exchange. An objective analyst such as Jean Bouvier might well criticize Zola for treating too lightly Saccard's belief in the positive effects of purchasing Universelle stock shares in great number:

> Here the formulation lends itself, at the very least,
> to confusion: the unbought shares cannot serve as a
> "battle reserve." . . . When a firm does not sell the
> totality of its stock, a weakening of its actual re-
> sources results. What will it do to fight against a fall
> in the price of its shares on the stock exchange? It
> will buy its own shares on the market; its weakness
> will then become that much more serious. The no-
> tion of a "battle reserve" is thus totally inadequate.[21]

What Bouvier in his cool rationalism misses here is what he himself glimpsed in another context: the *necessary excess* of the speculative process captured so characteristically in *L'Argent*. Speculation beckons to the practitioner, inviting him to defy the limits of
objective reality, to fulfill the goal of absolute possession. It is a
game of boom or bust, necessarily pitting those who adopt one
stance against those who adopt another in a fight to the death. The
success of the bulls signals the bankruptcy of the bears, and vice
versa. By focusing solely on the opposition between the two groups,
one risks overlooking their enslavement to one another, their underlying sameness. They are both prey to the impulse toward excess that is the central characteristic of futures operations.

The passionate quest by Saccard to acquire all the signifiers, to
master the field, is not without resonances in the context of Zola's
own project: to represent the Second Empire in its entirety, to
saturate it, to assemble exhaustively the signifiers meant to denote
it. Zola's vast undertaking—the twenty volumes of the *Rougon-
Macquart*, the attempt to outdo Balzac writing on Restoration society—strangely parallels Saccard's all-englobing ambition. Here
the confrontation between Saccard and Gundermann assumes a new
significance. Gundermann belongs to a genealogy including Sandoz, the proponent of "scientific" writing, of the new positivism—just as Gundermann himself is the financial version of the
positivist. But we have seen how that positivism is put to the test
and, in the end, almost cedes in the face of the challenge presented
by Saccard. Although the "imaginative" speculator ultimately fails,
his seductive figure escapes the disaster, beckoning, nearly unscathed, seemingly ready to begin the adventure once again. In

the final analysis, Sandoz's famous remark "Allons travailler" ("Let's go to work"), with which *L'Oeuvre* closes (4:363), pales in contrast to the vigorous, flamboyant practice of Saccard. Would Zola really have us place the naturalist project under the sign of Sandoz and Gundermann or, on the contrary, under that of Saccard? Zola seems to lean ever more perilously toward an endorsement of Saccard as *L'Argent* draws to a conclusion. Moreover, Saccard's very failure to corner the market is in some sense emblematic of the impossibility of Zola's own project: his representation of Second Empire society is destined to fall short (or, if the reader will forgive the pun, he is destined to sell the empire short).

In this and the three preceding chapters, the reader has come full circle from the beginning of speculation under the Second Empire in *La Curée* to its disastrous conclusion in *L'Argent*. The evolution of this economic activity has been marked by increasing reliance upon the signifier (deeds, façades, fashion, stock shares) and by increasing involvement in the process on the part of a widening cross-section of the public. One must be careful, however, to avoid viewing the participation of a greater number of small capitalists in the domain of speculation as a democratization of the process. For Saccard has made it clear from the beginning that associating small investors in speculation is simply another way of manipulating them:

> Around him, the congestion on the pavement and
> the sidewalks continued, an uninterrupted flow of
> people, the eternal crowd to be exploited, tomor-
> row's shareholders. They could not pass in front of
> the great lottery of speculation [the stock exchange]
> without turning their heads, filled with desire and
> fear for what went on there, for the mystery of finan-
> cial transactions made all the more attractive for
> French brains by the fact that few among them fath-
> omed it. (5:49)

Unlike larger capitalists, these smaller investors understand nothing of the stock market and can be blindly drawn in by hardened speculators. Moreover, unlike the larger capitalists, who can bear the risks of speculation and find rebirth after every financial disaster (Saccard himself being the prime example), the disaster at the end of *L'Argent* spells doom for a whole group of "small investors," "retired concierges," "provincial retirees," and "country priests." Their discovery that the stock shares/signifiers they possess can suddenly lose all significance, all worth, from one day to the next is one from which they will not recover. The drama of ultimately empty signifiers irreparably sweeps away a whole class of small investors. From this point of view, the financial crisis at the end of *L'Argent* is quite comparable to the political disintegration of the empire in *La Débâcle*. At the very moment when the French army desperately needs a strong center of power around which to rally, it too discovers that the emperor—who aimlessly wanders to and fro, unable to locate the Prussian army—amounts to no more than a collection of signs of power that have already been emptied of significance. The army, like the "small speculators," will be swept away beyond recovery. The excess of signifiers in the stock market is matched by a similar excess in the political arena.

Closure

The confrontation between Saccard and Gundermann that seems to pit them as opponents in symmetrical opposition to one another reveals, in fact, that the two men are fundamentally similar because they are subsumed by the processes of the stock exchange. Just as the question of political opposition came up in the context of the stategies employed in the political domain, one might ask how a possible opposition to the economic practices described in preceding chapters might be structured. *L'Argent* contains an oppositional figure who merits scrutiny in this context, namely, Sigismond Busch. He is the brother of the Busch whom the reader has already met in his role as pursuer of defaulting debtors. Sigismond is a socialist theoretician. He lives in a room provided for him by his brother, from which, significantly enough, he has a view of the Paris stock exchange. In fact, it would be safe to say that he is the character in the novel who follows Saccard's rise and fall most closely: "I have followed your affairs with a passion. Yes! From this room, tucked away so quietly, I have studied their day-to-day development, and I am as familiar with them as you are" (5:283). If Sigismond is capable of setting out the laws of Saccard's activities and applauds him for his successes, he predicts his downfall as well: "Thus we have seen the form of wealth already change one time, when the value of land fell, when landed property—fields and woods—gave way to transferable industrial securities, to bonds and stock shares. And we are witnessing today the precocious senility of the latter, a kind of rapid depreciation, because it is certain that prices are falling" (5:285). But Saccard's collapse, far from appearing tragic to Sigismond, instead would signal the arrival of a form of socialism in which profit-making as the main social incentive would disappear. Thus, at the heart of a novel describing yet another scheme for financial exploitation, there is a passionate observer who devises and works for the theory of a society that would turn the very mechanism of speculation against itself. As Sigismond remarks to Saccard, "You seem absolutely not to realize that you are leading us directly to collectivism" (5:283). Moreover, the coming of the new society is inevitable, its outlines mathematically inscribed in notes written by Sigismond in preparation for his definitive work: "I've done my work, I'll leave my notes. . . . Everything is provided for, everything resolved. Sovereign justice, absolute bliss are finally here. It's there on paper, mathematical and definitive" (5:285–86).

Sigismond, it would appear, is rather directly at odds with Aristide, the latter a representative of the profit incentive driven to its exemplary limit, the former a theoretician of an economic system wherein such "barbaric" motives would be abolished. The apparent antagonism between the views of the two characters, however, is a pivotal motif of L'Argent that merits a more careful analysis. In the first place, as was indicated above, Sigismond is fascinated by Saccard's projects, and thus a level of complicity between the two figures is present from the very beginning. Their relationship becomes even more intriguing when one analyzes the manner in which the narrative structure of the novel links them together, for it soon becomes evident that Sigismond's theoretical progress is tied to the vicissitudes of Saccard's career. Indeed, Sigismond appears only three times in the text of L'Argent, but his entrances always occur at highly significant moments. In the very first chapter of the novel, as Saccard is only beginning to formulate vague plans for the founding of a bank, Aristide has occasion to request of Sigismond a translation of a letter from a Russian banker. At this point, the reader discovers that Sigismond is a disciple of Karl Marx and that he has remained in Paris following the exile of his master to London in 1848. Since that time he has been studying in an attempt to set forth the theory of a socialist society. As he himself admits, however, "the reorganization is not ready; we are still looking. I hardly sleep anymore; I spend my nights working" (5:46). The uncertain beginnings of Saccard's projects are paralleled by Sigismond's preliminary theoretical reflections. Later, when Saccard is master of the stock exchange and the Banque Universelle is at its apogee, the reader finds Aristide once again engaged in a conversation with Sigismond. This second meeting reveals a Sigismond who, simultaneously with Saccard's success, has finalized his theoretical edifice: "It's there on paper, mathematical and definitive" (5:286). Ultimately, the crash of Saccard's bank finds an echo in the abrupt end of Sigismond's own revolutionary plans. Caroline Hamelin visits Busch following Saccard's demise and witnesses Sigismond's final moments as he dies, the victim of tuberculosis. At the end of his life, Sigismond discovers the vicious nature of his brother's activities and despairs of publishing his finished notes: "So, in a little while when I'm dead, my brother will sell my papers, and I don't want that, I don't want it!" (5:391). Saccard's fall is clearly paralleled by Sigismond's own death.

The coincidences evident in the development of both characters are further reinforced by the progress of Sigismond's tuberculosis. At the first meeting between the two, Sigismond's disease is only in its beginning stages: the narrator calls attention to a worrisome cough. During their second meeting, it becomes evident that Sigismond is possessed of the euphoria characteristic of the advanced stages of tuberculosis, a euphoria that reflects both his delight at completing his theory and Saccard's confidence that the Banque Universelle will continue to advance. Finally, Sigismond's agony symbolically repeats the demise of both his own plans and those of Saccard. Sigismond and Aristide are further linked to one another by their relationship to Busch. Sigismond is totally dependent upon his brother for both food and living quarters. His research, as objective and impartial as it may appear, is in the end a function of Busch's good will. Much of Busch's effort throughout *L'Argent* is directed toward creating a similar relationship of dependence between himself and Saccard by means of a blackmail scheme which, he believes, would put Saccard at his mercy.

Such a series of narrative parallels cannot be ignored. The two characters seem radically opposed to one another, Saccard energetically espousing extreme capitalism and Sigismond just as fervently believing in the coming socialist revolution. In fact, their shared prophetic effervescence already suggests a sympathetic bond between them. What is even more striking upon reflection, however, is the conspicuous relationship between the contents of their respective doctrines. Sigismond formulates the goal of collectivism in a manner which recalls quite directly Saccard's ambition in his confrontation with Gundermann. As early as the first conversation between Aristide and Sigismond, the latter predicts the disappearance of the stock exchange in the following terms: "It will disappear of its own accord once the state has expropriated it and logically become the nation's sole universal bank [*universelle banque*]" (5:46).[1] Later Sigismond outlines the collectivist strategy directed against Saccard and his class of entrepreneurs in similar terms: "The collectivist state has only to do what you are doing, expropriate you en masse once you have expropriated one by one the small investors—and then fulfill the ambition of your unbounded dream. If I'm right, that dream is to absorb all the world's capital, to be the sole bank, the general depository of public wealth" (5:283). The utopian vision that the dying Sigismond develops for Caroline in terms of justice, happiness, cooperation, and freedom as the novel ends cannot disguise the violence and coercion implied by the collectivist program. As in the case of Saccard, it is imperative that Sigismond's state become the sole source and control of wealth, the universal bank.

One must not, however, insist on the similarities between the projects of these two characters to the point that one neglects important differences. There is indeed a fundamental difference between those projects that must be stressed here. In the case of Saccard, economic ambition appears in a practically pure form. If there are any political aspirations apparent in his activities, they are extremely limited.[2] For Sigismond, on the other hand, the economic domain is a tool for founding what amounts to a new political system. The present study began with an analysis of the figure of Napoleon III that attempted to expose the working of economic principles within the political domain beneath certain imperial trappings. In Sigismond one finds yet another form of the imbrication of economics and politics. His opposition to the regime rests on a theory that subordinates the social and political to the economic even more fully and consciously than is the case in the empire itself. Historical progress appears to be linked all the more strongly to the dominance of the economic mode. The success of the opposition represented by Sigismond would be tantamount to an extension of the politico-economic structure already implied by the empire, a reinforcement in important ways of certain abuses of the Bonapartist regime. Sigismond, then, is clearly a figure of closure. If events occur as he predicts, they will be marked by the seal of a distressing sameness. Sigismond's predicament recalls that of Etienne, who, by his very participation in an organized opposition, is constrained to assume the position of "counter-master," to perpetuate the structures of exploitation. The logic of the end of the *Rougon-Macquart* cycle becomes more evident in this light: to break the vicious circle, to explode an ever-tightening closure, there is but one solution—a debacle, a catastrophe that might create the conditions necessary for a new and different politico-economic structure to take form. If Zola's use of the Franco-Prussian War in *La Débâcle* is motivated by history, it most certainly results as well from these more profound blockages in the novelistic series.

The debacle is twofold. The financial catastrophe comes right before the politico-military defeat as a first stage and a necessary preparation for the collapse of the imperial regime. Whatever one might say concerning the historical anachronism of such an arrangement of the events, it serves as a means to underscore the social and political vision at the heart of the *Rougon-Macquart* cycle. Economic structures dominate the social forms analyzed in Zola's fictional series. It is impossible to understand political and social power in the series if one does not grasp and ultimately focus upon this fact. The two figures around which the present study has been organized, that of the emperor and that of the speculator, share a certain number of common and fundamental traits that suggestively illustrate the imbrication of politics and economics. Zola's description of French society in the second half of the nineteenth century contains at the fictional level many of the insights that appear in the great theoretical edifice of the same period, Marx's ¹⁷¹ *Capital*. I have attempted in my study to illustrate the complexity, richness, and coherence of the social vision created by Zola in the *Rougon-Macquart*. Any attempt to assess Zola's ideology in the *Rougon-Macquart* must avoid reductionism and account for that coherence.

Notes

Chapter 1: Political Representation

1. The monograph by Maurice Descotes entitled *Le Personnage de Na-poléon III dans "Les Rougon-Macquart"* (Archives des Lettres modernes 114 [1970]) does little more than furnish an inventory of the em-peror's appearances in the series. Jean Borie's *Zola et les mythes; ou, De la nausée au salut* (Paris: Seuil, 1971) makes some interesting re-marks concerning Napoleon III but does not pursue the subject in detail. The most pertinent observations concerning Napoleon III may be found in Naomi Schor, *Zola's Crowds* (Baltimore: Johns Hopkins University Press, 1978), pp. 112–14 and 143–44. See also Philippe Hamon, *Le Personnel du roman: Le Système des personnages dans "Les Rou-gon-Macquart" d'Emile Zola* (Geneva: Droz, 1983), pp. 62–63, 266–67.

2. Emile Zola, *Les Rougon-Macquart,* ed. Henri Mitterand, 5 vols. (Par-is: Gallimard, 1960–67), 2:85. References to the novels in the *Rou-gon-Macquart* series will be from this edition and will henceforth be identified by volume and page number in the text. Translations of Zola's text, as well as of other texts in French, are mine unless oth-erwise indicated.

3. Naomi Schor has focused on this scene (*Zola's Crowds,* pp. 143–44)

and compared the clothing advertisement to the Greek colossus functioning as mediator.

4. See Hamon, *Le Personnel du roman,* pp. 69–89, for a study of the importance of the *regardeur-voyeur* in naturalistic fiction.

5. Philippe Bonnefis in his recent *L'Innommable: Essai sur l'oeuvre de Zola* (Paris: SEDES, 1984) has argued that the question of the father and of genealogy is central to nineteenth-century thought. Napoleon III's search for legitimacy is most certainly related to this problematic.

6. Vincent Descombes, *Le Platonisme* (Paris: Presses Universitaires de France [PUF], 1971), p. 51.

7. Gilles Deleuze, *Logique du sens* (Paris: Minuit, 1969), pp. 295–96, 293, and 296.

8. Gilles Deleuze, *Différence et répétition* (Paris: PUF, 1972), p. 92.

9. Jeffrey Mehlman, *Revolution and Repetition: Marx/Hugo/Balzac* (Berkeley and Los Angeles: University of California Press, 1977), p. 15.

10. Karl Marx, *The Eighteenth Brumaire of Louis Bonaparte,* trans. Ben Fowkes, in *Surveys from Exile,* ed. David Fernbach (New York: Vintage Books, 1974), pp. 164 and 188.

11. Mehlman, *Revolution and Repetition,* p. 16.

12. Quoted by Mehlman, ibid., p. 20.

13. In describing Zola's technique of preventing the formulation of clear-cut political opinions concerning what is right or wrong, legitimate or not legitimate, Philippe Hamon remarks, "All the characters engaged in political action [in the *Rougon-Macquart* series] are 'right,' and the confrontations of and parallels in their principles often have the effect of ultimately dismissing both 'revolutionary' representations and those which protect and maintain a previously-established right." See *Texte et idéologie* (Paris: PUF, 1984), p. 214.

14. The point of view of the beholder, it may be recalled, is all-important in the definition of the simulacrum. Xavier Audouard writes: "Simulacra . . . and what are simulacra? They are not copies. They differ from the latter by the fact that they are constructions which include the *observer's viewing angle,* so that the illusion is produced from the *very point of view of the observer.*" "Le Simulacre," *Cahiers pour l'Analyse* 3 (1966): 63.

15. Jean-Joseph Goux, *Freud, Marx: Economie et symbolique* (Paris: Seuil, 1973), p. 85.

16. Goux has recently continued his analysis in a book on Gide's *Les Faux Monnayeurs* entitled *Les Monnayeurs du langage* (Paris: Galilée, 1984). See pp. 129–33 for comments concerning Zola's *L'Argent*, comments with which I do not fully agree for reasons that will become clear below.

17. Karl Marx, *Capital: A Critique of Political Economy*, trans. Ben Fowkes (New York: Vintage Books, 1977), 1:141–42.

18. Karl Marx, *A Contribution to the Critique of Political Economy*, trans. S. W. Ryazonskaya, ed. Maurice Dobbs (New York: International Publishers, 1970), p. 39.

19. Karl Marx, *Grundrisse: Foundations of the Critique of Political Economy*, trans. Martin Nicolaus (New York: Vintage Books, 1973), p. 145.

20. Marx, *Contribution*, p. 125.

21. Borie speaks of "the paradox of a work whose ambition is to reconstitute a period and a regime, but which nonetheless is situated in an *excentric* fashion in relation to that regime. In the end, the most historical and political novel of the series is the first, *La Fortune des Rougon*, which hardly presents History other than through its distant repercussions in a small, provincial village." *Zola et les mythes*, p. 70.

22. Michel Aglietta and André Orléan, *La Violence de la monnaie* (Paris: PUF, 1982), p. 17.

23. Ibid., p. 33.

24. Louis Marin, *Le Portrait du roi* (Paris: Minuit, 1981), p. 157. See also Marc Shell, *The Economy of Literature* (Baltimore: Johns Hopkins University Press, 1978), pp. 11–14, for further discussion of this subject.

25. Marin, *Le Portrait du roi*, p. 158.

Chapter 2: Representational Strategies

1. A reference to the tale of the emperor's new clothes is irresistible in this context. It has much to say about the moment when transcendence suddenly vanishes.

2. The shadow motif has further ramifications to which I shall return in a moment. Naomi Schor (*Zola's Crowds*, pp. 112–14) has also focused on this motif in *La Débâcle* in a reading of Napoleon III based on remarks by Gilles Deleuze in *Logique du sens*. The emperor is a constantly displaced element in the system of the battle at Sedan

and, as such, is a function which succeeds in bringing together the disparate elements into a certain unity. Schor's insistence upon the fact that the emperor has no space, no place, and that he circulates constantly are points which are equally fundamental to my own analysis.

3. Schor, *Zola's Crowds*, pp. 112–14.

4. Philippe Hamon has called Zola's Napoleon III a sphinx and has demonstrated how in the *Rougon-Macquart* power belongs to those who are informed and who are able to maintain others in a state of ignorance. See *Le Personnel du roman*, pp. 305–7.

5. Michel Serres, *Genèse* (Paris: Grasset, 1981), p. 57. Serres plays with the word *persona* in this passage. He uses *personne* in French, which also means "no one."

6. Not only does the motif of the mask recur, but the significance of the original scene between Nana and Muffat is later reemphasized when it is replayed, albeit in less perfect form. After a stormy rupture between Nana and the count, Muffat returns to Nana with the intention of asking her to come back with him. The scene takes place once again in Nana's backstage dressing room amid creams, make-up, and provocative scents. The symmetry involved here is not one of chance.

7. It is no coincidence that both moments of unmasking are provoked by diseases. "Punitive notions of disease have a long history," notes Susan Sontag in her *Illness as Metaphor* (New York: Farrar, Strauss and Giroux, 1978), p. 57. Mme de Merteuil is one of Nana's illustrious predecessors. Although Napoleon III's illness is a "historical fact," it bears mentioning that the first Napoleon contracted cancer and that contemporaries associated the disease with the political defeat he suffered.

8. David Baguley, "Les Paradis perdus: Espace et regard dans *La Conquête de Plassans* de Zola," *Nineteenth-Century French Studies* 9 (Fall-Winter 1980–81): 80–92.

9. Ibid., p. 85. Baguley neglects to point out that the importance of seeing without being seen as a political strategy has been the subject of many recent analyses of political power. See, for example, Marc Shell, *The Economy of Literature*, or Michel Foucault, *Surveiller et punir* (Paris: Gallimard, 1975).

10. For an analysis of the topology of the three houses in *La Conquête* (Mouret, Rastoil, and Péqueur des Saulaies) and the alley that joins them together, see Michel Serres, *Feux et signaux de brume: Zola* (Paris: Grasset, 1975), pp. 244–51.

11. Paule Lejeune, *"Germinal": Un Roman antipeuple* (Paris: Nizet, 1978); André Vial, *"Germinal" et le "socialisme" de Zola* (Paris: Editions Sociales, 1975).

12. Sandy Petrey, "Discours social et littéraire dans *Germinal,*" *Littérature* 22 (May 1976): 59–74.

13. Henri Mitterand, "Le Savoir et l'imaginaire: *Germinal* et les idéologies," and "L'idéologie et le mythe: *Germinal* et les fantasmes," in *Le Discours du roman* (Paris: PUF, 1980), pp. 123–39 and 140–49.

14. Michel Serres, *The Parasite,* trans. Lawrence R. Schehr (Baltimore: Johns Hopkins University Press, 1982), p. 59.

15. The word *contre-maître* normally means "foreman"—i.e., the person in charge of organizing a team of workers at the behest of management. Serres insists on the literal meaning of the expression, "counter-master," in order to develop structural similarities he detects between the roles and positions of both "masters."

16. In an article entitled "Le Trou et les bouches noires: Parole, société, révolution dans *Germinal,*" *Littérature* 24 (December 1976): 11–39, Claude Duchet studies language and the act of speaking in *Germinal* and comes to conclusions related to my own. He demonstrates that the miners have no rational language in the novel, and when Etienne and others try to find one, they can only insert themselves into the circuit of bourgeois language. There is no "parole ouvrière," only a language always recuperated by the class in the position of mastery.

17. The French expression meaning "corporation," *société anonyme,* admirably exposes the absence of a focal point of authority and responsibility upon which I am insisting here.

18. Henri Mitterand, "Notes sur l'idéologie du mythe dans *Germinal,*" *La Pensée,* no. 156 (April 1971): 85. This article is reproduced, although in modified form, in *Le Discours du roman* under the title "L'idéologie et le mythe: *Germinal* et les fantasmes" (see n. 13, above). I quote from *La Pensée* because I think the formulation is clearer.

19. Mitterand, "Le Savoir et l'imaginaire," p. 130.

20. Goux, *Freud, Marx,* pp. 68–69.

21. The term *béance* is used by both Duchet, "Le Trou et les bouches noires," p. 39, and Mitterand, "Le Savoir et l'imaginaire," p. 139.

Chapter 3: Deeds and Incest

1. Samuel Weber, *The Legend of Freud* (Minneapolis: University of Minnesota Press, 1982).

2. Claude Duchet, Preface to Emile Zola, *La Curée* (Paris: Garnier Flammarion, 1970), p. 18.

3. This act of taking possession by pounding the pavement with one's boots is a motif to which Zola returns in *L'Oeuvre*.

4. The reader later encounters gold coins again, this time scattered around the stage for one of the tableaux in M. Hupel de la Noue's *Echo et Narcisse*. See below.

5. Michel Foucault's analysis of the concept of the panopticon in *Surveiller et punir* comes naturally to mind in this context.

6. I say "so-called" because it is difficult, if not impossible, to determine what is "ordinary" or "normal" in the domain of exchange, in short, what constitutes "regular trading or investment." This debate is central to Zola's *L'Argent,* and I shall have more to say concerning it when I turn my attention to that novel.

7. As became evident earlier, such a strategy also exposes the emperor to the dangers of inflation and catastrophic devaluation.

8. Philippe Hamon has had much to say about the rhetorical and semiotic techniques of Zola's writing in analyses found in *Le Personnel du roman* and *Texte et idéologie*.

9. Serres, *Feux et signaux de brume,* p. 252.

10. Brian Nelson realizes that this is so in his "Speculation and Dissipation: A Reading of Zola's *La Curée*," *Essays in French Literature* 14 (November 1977): 1–33. However, he does not pursue the observation he makes on page 6 of his article: "Speculation and incest are closely related on the level of the narrative: . . . the theme of incest interlocks with the eventual transfer of property to Saccard."

11. Of course, the real estate in question will be in Renée's name, ostensibly out of Saccard's hands, but he is not in the habit of being deterred by such details.

12. For a thorough study of this material, see Sandy Petrey, "Stylistics and Society in *La Curée*," *MLN* 89 (1974): 626–40.

13. Hamon, *Le Personnel du roman*, p. 263.

14. Saccard's sensitivity to language is apparent in the oft-cited passage in which he settles on the name Saccard as a pseudonym (1:364): all authors know the importance of the names of characters in their books. Hamon's *Le Personnel du roman* and Philippe Bonnefis's *L'Innommable* both contain extensive reflections on Zola himself as creator of names and of the importance he bestowed upon this activity.

15. Lucien Dällenbach, in "L'Oeuvre dans l'oeuvre chez Zola," *Le Naturalisme,* Colloque de Cérisy (Paris: Union Générale d'Editions, 1978), p. 137, expresses an interesting thesis concerning the theatrical *mises en abyme* in *La Curée.* "Without a doubt, these two representations *en abyme* in *La Curée* (*Phèdre* and the *anti-Phèdre* illustrated by 'the poem about the beautiful Narcissus and the nymphe Echo') serve not only to justify the use of a literary genre still not quite legitimate at the time—the novel—but they also attempt to justify the recourse to the *dramatic* novel which the two productions are destined precisely to render possible by contamination." The dramatic "contamination" of *La Curée* is perhaps wider than Dällenbach suggests: the description of Saccard's (and Larsonneau's) praxis, as we have seen, is also expressed in terms of dramatic conventions.

16. Needless to say, the accumulation suggested in this passage can only lead to a mixed architectural style that mimics numerous other styles: "It was a small-scale rendering of the new Louvre, one of the most characteristic examples of the Napoleon III style, that opulent crossbreed of all styles" (1:332). This remark is interesting in light of the analysis of the figure of Napoleon III. Just as the emperor circulates among different positions without occupying any one definitively, so does the architectural style he imposes. And the result is none too pleasing to the eye.

17. Philippe Hamon, in "Zola, romancier de la transparence," *Europe,* nos. 468–69 (1968): 385–91, identified the "transparency complex" in Zola's writing evident here and also massively present in *Au Bonheur des Dames,* in which a major descriptive trait of Mouret's store is its great "glaces sans tain" (display windows) through which the inside of the store may be seen.

18. The theme of the façade might well be seen as a metaphor for the reading of Zola's text. The striking and brilliant detail which fascinates and seduces Zola as a writer is, in a sense, "superficial"—not

because it is unimportant, but because it is at the surface in the more literal sense. Instead of leading the reader to a more "profound" truth, it overwhelms him, blinds him with its brilliance, tantalizes him with bits and pieces, with glimpses of something within—which he can never quite grasp, because it is not really there. In other words, the proliferation of description which marks the naturalist text accomplishes quite the opposite of what it theoretically sets out to do (i.e., to represent the "real" or the "truth").

19. Jean Borie, in *Zola et les mythes,* correctly points out that "whatever might be the speculators' zone of activity, their efforts tend almost always to be concretized in some kind of building" (p. 174). For Saccard, however, real estate is not a crowning touch, but rather, the very basis of his activity.

20. Frank Norris, *The Pit* (New York: Grosset and Dunlap, 1903), pp. 87, 191.

21. Howard Horwitz, " 'To Find the Value of X': *The Pit* as Renunciation of Romance," in *American Realism: New Essays,* ed. Eric Sundquist (Baltimore: Johns Hopkins University Press, 1982), pp. 218–19.

22. I do not wish to belabor the *mise en abyme* problematic which has been amply discussed by various Zola critics and which is so blatantly employed by the novelist. Nevertheless, I would note that both characters, Echo and Narcissus, enter directly into the context of sameness, of refusal of difference that runs through the speculative and incestuous strains of *La Curée.* There is a veritable fear of difference that plagues the novel and that has been interpreted by Lucien Dällenbach as an attempt on Zola's part to prevent polysemy, to preclude divergent readings. See "L'Oeuvre dans l'oeuvre chez Zola." The *mise en abyme* itself seems clearly to be just another strategy of sameness in a novel full of such strategies.

Chapter 4: The Play of Fashion

1. See the documentary material presented by Mitterand in the Pléiade edition of the *Rougon-Macquart* for illustrations of Zola's creative process.

2. Schor, *Zola's Crowds,* p. 153.

3. Serres, *Feux et signaux de brume,* p. 287.

4. Ibid.

5. Ibid.

6. Michael Miller in his study of the Bon Marché calls attention to the fact (left unsaid by Zola) that rationalization of the street layout in Paris was accomplished by a rationalization and improvement of the system of public transportation. See *The Bon Marché: Bourgeois Culture and the Department Store, 1869–1920* (Princeton: Princeton University Press, 1981), pp. 35–36.

7. For an analysis of the invasions of sanctuaries by the street—i.e., by outside forces—see Borie, *Zola et les mythes,* pp. 151–68. Mouret's progress may be gauged by his increasing success in provoking such an invasion.

8. Alain Plessis, *De la fête impériale au mur des fédérés* (Paris: Seuil, 1973), p. 162.

9. Marx, *The Eighteenth Brumaire,* p. 198.

10. René Girard, *Des Choses cachées depuis la fondation du monde* (Paris: Grasset, 1978), pp. 15–17.

11. Ibid., p. 319.

12. The analysis of desire in psychoanalytic terms and particularly in Lacanian terms could reveal as well—via a different route—the efficacy of the fashion mechanism as a domain for interaction with the other. Psychoanalysis insists on the open-ended nature of desire. If there could be a conceivable end to desire, its ultimate fulfillment, then desire would collapse. The subject would be reunited with that which she or he lacks. But since that lack is the fundamental characteristic of the human condition, resulting from the splitting off from the mother and the insertion into society (the move from the Imaginary into the Symbolic in Lacanian terms), the only conceivable end to desire is in death. Lacan clearly distinguishes between *need* and *desire* in order to make this point. A need has a definite object with which it can be fulfilled; there are as many needs as there are objects capable of fulfilling them (hence, for example, the grammatical possibility of using the indefinite article *a* with the noun *need*). Desire has no object (and in psychoanalysis there is never *a* desire): it is more like a general interactive structure through which the subject relates to the other. The fashion item could, in this context, be analyzed as a

mediating object in the ongoing attempt to situate oneself with respect to the other: an ersatz object only temporarily effective until desire drives the subject on to something else. The fashion item is thus never an end in itself, but always rather an infinitely substitutable symbolic object—one would be tempted to say infinitely renewable. With this in mind, one could then argue that judicious manipulation of fashion is a continuously renewable source of exchange from which profit can surely be drawn in the economic domain.

13. Jean-Pierre Dupuy, "Le Signe et l'envie," in Jean-Pierre Dupuy and Paul Dumouchel, *L'Enfer des choses: René Girard et la logique de l'économie* (Paris: Seuil, 1979), pp. 17–134.

14. René Girard, *Deceit, Desire, and the Novel*, trans. Yvonne Freccero (Baltimore: Johns Hopkins Press, 1965), p. 14. Translation slightly modified.

15. Schor, *Zola's Crowds*, p. 158.

16. Theodor Adorno, *Minima Moralia: Reflections from Damaged Life*, trans. E.F.N. Jephcott (London: NLB, 1974), p. 119.

17. In much the same way as Claude Lantier's paintings in *L'Oeuvre*, one might add.

18. Theodor Adorno, *Prisms*, trans. Samuel and Shierry Weber (Cambridge: MIT Press, 1981), p. 82.

19. See Rosa Luxemburg, *The Accumulation of Capital*, trans. Agnes Schwarzschild (London: Routledge and Kegan Paul, 1951), p. 365: "Capitalism in its full maturity also depends in all respects on non-capitalist strata and social organizations existing side by side with it."

20. Hannah Arendt, *The Origins of Totalitarianism* (New York: Harcourt Brace Jovanovich, 1973), p. 148.

21. Luxemburg, *Accumulation of Capital*, p. 446.

Chapter 5: Taking Stock

1. Jean Bouvier, *Initiation au vocabulaire et aux mécanismes économiques contemporains (XIXe-XXe siècles)* (Paris: SEDES, 1972), pp. 42–45. See also Jean Bouvier, *Naissance d'une banque: Le Crédit Lyonnais* (Paris: Flammarion, 1968), pp. 101–3, for a description of the effects of

this crisis on the Crédit Lyonnais. Bouvier addresses the general problem of historical anachronism in *L'Argent* in an article devoted exclusively to that work. He argues that although Zola's description is based on the economic situation of the 1880s in France, the differences between the earlier period (1864–68) and the later period are not fundamental. See *"L'Argent*: Roman et réalité,*"* *Europe,* nos. 468–69 (April–May, 1968): 56.

2. The reader will recall that the novel following the financial disaster recounted in *L'Argent* is *La Débâcle,* in which the military and political disintegration of the empire is described.

3. It is worth noting once again Saccard's prodigious attention to names. This applies also to the name of the bank itself, which Saccard finds in a moment of inspiration: " 'The Banque Universelle,' he repeated ceaselessly to himself while he was dressing, 'the Banque Universelle. It's simple, it's grand, it encompasses everything, it covers the world!' " (5:82).

4. Arendt, *The Origins of Totalitarianism,* p. 150.

5. In *Capital,* Marx explains this process as the creation of universal money that occurs when economic exchanges reach the international level and are emptied of parochial characteristics. "When money leaves the home sphere of circulation, it strips off the local garbs which it there assumes, of a standard of prices, of coins, of tokens, and of a symbol of value, and returns to its original form of bullion" (1:142). It is fitting that a novel on nascent imperialism, *L'Argent,* contains a clear allusion to a process related to the international stage of capitalism.

6. See Serres, *Feux et signaux de brume,* for a development of this parallel.

7. This aspect of Saccard's theory of speculation alludes to the famous "démocratisation du crédit" that was an economic catchword in the second half of the nineteenth century in France. The problem of how to draw savings out of the proverbial "stocking" and into circulation was finally successfully addressed by the formation of investment banks, i.e., banks like the Banque Universelle of *L'Argent.* On this problem see Jean Bouvier, *Etudes sur le krach de l'Union Générale (1878–1885)* (Paris: PUF, 1960), p. 43.

8. It is important to note that the architectural bastardization apparent

in the Parc Monceau mansion in *La Curée* is once again evident in the Universelle's new rue de Londres headquarters. As the narrator puts it, "The façade rose up floridly decorated, looking simultaneously like a temple and a café-concert" (5:228).

9. The force of the Girardian concept of mimetic desire becomes quite evident in this context. Girard has always insisted upon the secondary nature of the object desired in the triangular structure. Once the two rivals identify each other, the gaze of each is riveted upon the other, the actions of each governed by the other. The object originally at stake was perhaps never at stake at all, was, in other words, only a catalyst and destined rapidly to be forgotten. This structure is graphically illustrated in the stock market, where the success of investment strategies lies in absolute imitation of the other—a confrontation for mastery in a domain emptied of objects or, to state it in another way, filled with fantastically fungible paper goods.

10. Hamon, *Texte et idéologie*, p. 188.

11. Marx, *The Eighteenth Brumaire*, p. 237.

12. Ibid., p. 191.

13. Edmond Théry, *La France économique et financière pendant le dernier quart de siècle* (Paris: Economiste Européen, 1900), pp. 198–99.

14. A later writer was to call this episode "a kind of archetypal or standard scandal upon which future catastrophes of the same kind would inevitably be modeled." See Jules Bertrand, *Les Dessous de la finance* (Paris: Editions Jules Tallandier, 1954), p. 285.

15. Théry, *La France économique et financière*, p. 226.

16. Claudio Jannet, *Le Capital, la spéculation et la finance au XIXe siècle* (Paris: Librairie Plon, 1892), p. 155.

17. Walter Benn Michaels, "Dreiser's *Financier*: The Man of Business as a Man of Letters," in *American Realism: New Essays,* ed. Eric J. Sundquist (Baltimore: Johns Hopkins University Press, 1982), pp. 278–94.

18. Bouvier, *Etudes sur le krach de l'Union Générale*, p. 28.

19. Gaston Défossé, *La Bourse des valeurs* (Paris: PUF, 1959), p. 63.

20. Ibid., p. 64.

21. Bouvier, *"L'Argent,"* p. 60.

Closure

1. An almost imperceptible inversion would suffice to transform the "universelle banque" into the "Banque Universelle."
2. One might perhaps qualify as political Saccard's campaign to limit the influence of the Jewish financial milieu in French government affairs. This is, however, quite secondary to his desire for financial mastery.

185

Selected Bibliography

Adorno, Theodor. *Minima Moralia: Reflections from Damaged Life*. Trans. E. F. N. Jephcott. London: NLB, 1974.

—————. *Prisms*. Trans. Samuel and Shierry Weber. Cambridge: MIT Press, 1981.

Aglietta, Michel, and André Orléan. *La Violence de la monnaie*. Paris: Presses Universitaires de France, 1982.

Arendt, Hannah. *The Origins of Totalitarianism*. New York: Harcourt Brace Jovanovich, 1973.

Audouard, Xavier. "Le Simulacre." *Cahiers pour l'Analyse* 3 (1966): 84–89.

Baguley, David. "Les Paradis perdus: Espace et regard dans *La Conquête de Plassans* de Zola." *Nineteenth-Century French Studies* 9 (Fall–Winter 1980–81): 80–92.

Bertrand, Jules. *Les Dessous de la finance*. Paris: Editions Jules Tallandier, 1954.

Bonnefis, Philippe. *L'Innommable: Essai sur l'oeuvre de Zola*. Paris: SEDES, 1984.

Borie, Jean. *Zola et les mythes; ou, De la nausée au salut*. Paris: Seuil, 1971.

Bouvier, Jean. *Etudes sur le krach de l'Union Générale (1878–1885)*. Paris: Presses Universitaires de France, 1960.

———. *Initiation au vocabulaire et aux mécanismes économiques contemporains (XIXe–XXe siècles)*. Paris: SEDES, 1972.

———. *"L'Argent: Roman et réalité." Europe,* nos. 468–69 (April–May 1968): 54–63.

———. *Naissance d'une banque: Le Crédit Lyonnais*. Paris: Flammarion, 1968.

Dällenbach, Lucien. "L'Oeuvre dans l'oeuvre chez Zola." In *Le Naturalisme,* pp. 125–39, Colloque de Cérisy. Paris: Union Générale d'Editions, 1978.

Défossé, Gaston. *La Bourse des valeurs*. Paris: Presses Universitaires de France, 1959.

Deleuze, Gilles. *Différence et répétition*. Paris: Presses Universitaires de France, 1972.

———. *Logique du sens*. Paris: Minuit, 1969.

Descombes, Vincent. *Le Platonisme*. Paris: Presses Universitaires de France, 1971.

Descotes, Maurice. *Le Personnage de Napoléon III dans "Les Rougon-Macquart."* Archives des Lettres modernes 114 (1970).

Duchet, Claude. Preface to *La Curée,* by Emile Zola. Paris: Garnier Flammarion, 1970.

———. "Le Trou et les bouches noires: Parole, société, révolution dans *Germinal." Littérature* 24 (December 1976): 11–39.

Dupuy, Jean-Pierre. "Le Signe et l'envie." In Jean-Pierre Dupuy and Paul Dumouchel, *L'Enfer des choses: René Girard et la logique de l'économie,* pp. 17–134. Paris: Seuil, 1979.

Foucault, Michel. *Surveiller et punir*. Paris: Gallimard, 1975.

Girard, René. *Des Choses cachées depuis la fondation du monde*. Paris: Grasset, 1978.

———. *Mensonge romantique et vérité romanesque*. Paris: Grasset, 1961.

Goux, Jean-Joseph. *Freud, Marx: Economie et symbolique*. Paris: Seuil, 1973.

———. *Les Monnayeurs du langage*. Paris: Galilée, 1984.

Hamon, Philippe. *Le Personnel du roman: Le Système des personnages dans "Les Rougon-Macquart" d'Emile Zola*. Geneva: Droz, 1983.

———. *Texte et idéologie*. Paris: Presses Universitaires de France, 1984.

———. "Zola, romancier de la transparence." *Europe,* nos. 468–69 (1968): 385–91.

Horowitz, Howard. "'To Find the Value of *X*': *The Pit* as Renunciation of Romance." In *American Realism: New Essays,* ed. Eric J. Sundquist, pp. 215–37. Baltimore: Johns Hopkins University Press, 1982.

Hugo, Victor. *Poésie.* Ed. Bernard Leuillot. Vol. 1. Paris: Seuil, 1972.

Jannet, Claudio. *Le Capital, la spéculation et la finance au XIXe siècle.* Paris: Librairie Plon, 1892.

Lejeune, Paule. *"Germinal": Un Roman antipeuple.* Paris: Nizet, 1978.   189

Luxemburg, Rosa. *The Accumulation of Capital.* Trans. Agnes Schwartschild. London: Routledge and Kegan Paul, 1951.

Marin, Louis. *Le Portrait du roi.* Paris: Minuit, 1981.

Marx, Karl. *Capital: A Critique of Political Economy.* Trans. Ben Fowkes. Vol. 1. New York: Vintage Books, 1977.

————. *A Contribution to the Critique of Political Economy.* Trans. S. W. Ryazonskaya and ed. Maurice Dobbs. New York: International Publishers, 1970.

————. *The Eighteenth Brumaire of Louis Bonaparte.* Trans. Ben Fowkes. In *Surveys from Exile,* ed. David Fernbach, pp. 143–249, New York: Vintage Books, 1974.

————. *Grundrisse: Foundations of the Critique of Political Economy.* Trans. Martin Nicolaus. New York: Vintage Books, 1973.

Mehlman, Jeffrey. *Revolution and Repetition: Marx/Hugo/Balzac.* Berkeley and Los Angeles: University of California Press, 1977.

Michaels, Walter Benn. "Dreiser's *Financier:* The Man of Business as a Man of Letters." In *American Realism: New Essays,* ed. Eric J. Sundquist, pp. 278–94. Baltimore: Johns Hopkins University Press, 1982.

Miller, Michael. *The Bon Marché: Bourgeois Culture and the Department Store, 1869–1920.* Princeton: Princeton University Press, 1981.

Mitterand, Henri. *Le Discours du roman.* Paris: Presses Universitaires de France, 1980.

————. "Notes sur l'idéologie du mythe dans *Germinal.*" *La Pensée,* no. 156 (April 1971): 81–86.

Nelson, Brian. "Speculation and Dissipation: A Reading of Zola's *La Curée.*" *Essays in French Literature* 14 (November 1977): 1–33.

Norris, Frank. *The Pit.* New York: Grosset and Dunlap, 1903.

Petrey, Sandy. "Discours social et littéraire dans *Germinal.*" *Littérature* 22 (May 1976): 59–74.

————. "Stylistics and Society in *La Curée.*" *MLN* 89 (1974): 626–40.

Plessis, Alain. *De la fête impériale au mur des fédérés.* Paris: Seuil, 1973.

Schor, Naomi. *Zola's Crowds.* Baltimore: Johns Hopkins University Press, 1978.

Serres, Michel. *Feux et signaux de brume: Zola.* Paris: Grasset, 1975.

————. *Genèse.* Paris: Grasset, 1981.

190   ————. *Le Parasite.* Paris: Grasset, 1980.

Shell, Marc. *The Economy of Literature.* Baltimore: Johns Hopkins University Press, 1978.

Sontag, Susan. *Illness as Metaphor.* New York: Farrar, Strauss, and Giroux, 1978.

Théry, Edmond. *La France économique et financière pendant le dernier quart de siècle.* Paris: Economiste Européen, 1900.

Vial, André. *"Germinal" et le "socialisme" de Zola.* Paris: Editions Sociales, 1975.

Weber, Samuel. *The Legend of Freud.* Minneapolis: University of Minnesota Press, 1982.

Zola, Emile. *Oeuvres complètes.* Ed. Henri Mitterand. 15 vols. Paris: Cercle du Livre Précieux, 1966–69.

————. *Les Rougon-Macquart: Histoire naturelle et sociale d'une famille sous le Second Empire.* Ed. Henri Mitterand. Bibliothèque de la Pléiade. 5 vols. Paris: Gallimard, 1960–67. (This edition is cited in the text.)

Index

Adorno, Theodor, 116, 122
Advertisement: in journalism, 135–37; as strategy of speculation, 116–17, 135–140
Aglietta, Michel, 20
Animism, Freud's theory of, 60–61
Arendt, Hannah, 124, 130

Baguley, David, 40–41
Balzac, Honoré de, xii, 66; *La Comédie humaine,* ix
Baptismal ceremony, of Napoleon III's son, 4–6, 10, 21–23
Barthes, Roland, x
Bear, in stock market, 142, 159, 163. *See also* Bull
Bonapartism, 8–12, 20, 29, 108–9, 170
Borie, Jean, 19
Bouvier, Jean, 156, 162–63
Bull, in stock market, 142, 163. *See also* Bear
Butor, Michel, ix

Capitalism: American, xi, 152–53; and imperialism, 123–24, 129–30; in relation to socialism, 167–70
Commodity: and exchange, 14–17, 67–68, 113–14; fashion, 118, 122; fragmentation of, 110–12, 116; gold as, 22, 26, 53, 132; materiality of, 109–10, 119, 126–27, 131, 152; as mirror, 35, 73; and money, 99–100; production of, 96
Confrontation, political, 46–53; one against many, 47–48; one-to-one, 47–49, 51. *See also* Opposition
Coronation, of Napoleon I, 5–7
Crowd, 2; and confrontation, 46; and fashion, 112, 115, 118; as political weapon, 108–9; and speculation, 101–2, 108

Deed, as speculative artifice, 69–71, 74–78
Défossé, Gaston, 158–59
Deleuze, Gilles, 6–7
Descombes, Vincent, 6–7
Desire, mimetic, 112–14

Dream, Freudian interpretation of, 59–61, 64
Dreiser, Theodore: *The Financier,* xii, 152–53
Duchet, Claude, 62
Dupuy, Jean-Pierre, 113–14

Engels, Friedrich, 9
Equivalent, general, 15, 73; Nana as, 35, 39; Napoleon III as, 19, 22, 68. *See also* Equivalent, universal
Equivalent, universal, x, 15–19; gold as, 16–17, 22; as mediator, 53; phallus as, 55–56; as transcendental, 21, 26. *See also* Equivalent, general
Exchange: as acquisitive violence, 20–21; economic, 14–18; and mimesis, 113–14; structure of, x, 20–21, 24, 67–68

Façade, 31; as advertisement, x, 104–7, 137–38; and credit, 85–86, 90–91; as signifier of wealth, 83–87, 95, 100. *See also* Mask
Fashion, 110; and advertising techniques, 116–17; definition of, 112, 120; and mimesis, 114–15, 118; and process of signification, 120; and social position of women, 121–23
Fetishism, 21–22, 24
Flaubert, Gustave: *L'Education sentimentale,* 38
Freud, Sigmund, 59–64; interpretation of dreams in, 59–61; narcissism in, 59–61, 64; theory of animism in, 60–61; *Totem and Taboo,* 60
Futures operations: and logic of speculation, 158–59, 163; as test case for speculation, 150–51, 153

Genealogy, 6, 25, 51. *See also* Legitimacy; Lineage
Gide, André: *Les Faux Monnayeurs,* xii
Girard, René: *Deceit, Desire, and the Novel,* 112–13
Gold, x; as commodity, 26, 53, 132; as image of speculation, 63, 100; as mediator, 17, 20; as money, 14, 16–17, 66–67; Nana as, 40; as signifier of wealth, 83–84, 94–95; standard, xii; transcendental character of, 17, 53; as universal equivalent, x, 16–17, 22, 39
Goux, Jean-Joseph, 55; *Freud, Marx: Economie et symbolique,* 14–15, 18, 21–22; *Les Monnayeurs du langage,* xii

Hamon, Philippe, 78
Haussmann, Baron, x, 2, 89, 107–8, 145
Horwitz, Howard, 92
Hugo, Victor, 9

Imperialism. *See* Capitalism
Incest, 58; and speculation, 73–77
Inflation, 21; in the political sphere, 27

Jannet, Claudio: *Le Capital au XIXe siècle,* 149–54

Legitimacy, x, 9; and illegitimacy, 13; of Napoleon III, 5–6, 25; in the Rougon-Macquart family, 13. *See also* Genealogy; Lineage
Lejeune, Paule, 43, 54
Lineage, 5–7, 13, 21. *See also* Genealogy; Legitimacy
Luxemburg, Rosa, 124

Marin, Louis, 23
Marriage, as speculative operation, 74–78

Marx, Karl, x, 20, 26, 35, 53–54, 66, 146, 168; *Capital*, 15, 17–18, 55, 67, 73, 171; *The Eighteenth Brumaire of Louis Bonaparte*, 8–9, 14, 19, 108–9; *Grundrisse*, 67, 87; *Lumpenproletariat*, 108

Mask, 29–38; and general equivalent, 30; makeup as, 36–38; Nana's skin as, 34–35, 41; Napoleon III's, 28–30, 72; and neutrality, 41–42; and unmasking, 30–31, 38. *See also* Shadow

Medallion: and money, 23–25; and political representation, 23–25

Mehlman, Jeffrey, 8

Michaels, Walter Benn, xi-xii, 152–53

Mimesis: of appropriation, 112–14; and exchange, 113–14; and fashion, 114–15; in the stock market, 140–41

Mitterand, Henri, 45, 54–56, 98

Money: genesis of, 14–18, 20–21, 54–55, 66; and liquidity, 88–89, 95, 133–34; as metal and means of exchange, 128–29; and process of symbolization, 18; as a social institution, 20–21; and speculation, 68, 73, 87; and turnover, 97–99, 111, 119

Myth: Napoleonic, 1, 5; and working class ideology, 55

Napoleon I, 3–4, 9; and relationship to Napoleon III, 5–7; and renovations of Paris, 64

Napoleon III, x, 1–26, 170; as actor, 30, 33; description of, 28–29; as empty sign, 28, 83; as general equivalent, 18–19, 22, 28, 72, 87–88; as master of signs, 72; and narcissism, 64–66; as parasite, 146, 151; and relationship to Napoleon I, 5–7;

and renovations of Paris, 61–66, 68–69, 104–5, 107–9; as shadow, 27–28, 31–33, 36; as simulacrum, 30; and the Society of 10 December, 108–9; spectrality of, 27–28; as speculator, 66, 68, 109; transcendence of, 32

Narcissism, 59–61, 64, 74, 107; and politics of Napoleon III, 64–66

Naturalism: American, xi, 152–53; as corner on the market, 163–64; as speculative enterprise, 81, 171–72

Norris, Frank: *The Pit*, 92–93, 152, 162; *The Responsibilities of the Novelist*, 92

Opposition, xi; political, in *Germinal*, 44–56; republic/empire, 12; Saccard/Busch, 166–70; Saccard/Gundermann, 155–62, 166. *See also* Confrontation; Symmetry

Orléan, André, 20

Petrey, Sandy, 45

Platonism, 7

Pretender: Napoleon III as, 5–6; in Plato, 7. *See also* Simulacrum

Representation: corporative, 50–51; economic, 51; of Napoleon I, 9; political, 1–25, 30; in political confrontations, 46–56

Republicanism, 10–12, 20, 29

Rivalry: between Antoine and Pierre Rougon, 12–13; of commodities, 15; dialectic of, in Plato, 7; between exchanging parties, 20–21, 113–14; between Saccard and Gundermann, 157–62

Schor, Naomi, 28, 101, 115

Serres, Michel, 29–30, 33, 73,

102–3; *Le Parasite,* 45–46, 48–
49

Shadow: Faujas as, 41; and Nana's
skin, 36; Napoleon III as, 27–
28, 31–33, 41. *See also* Mask

Shell, Marc: *The Economy of Literature,* xi

Simulacrum, 5–7, 9–12, 13–14,
22, 29–30, 146

Socialism: in relation to capitalism,
167–70; Zola's, 44

Space: in *Au Bonheur des Dames,*
102–6; logic of, 103; in renovations of Paris, 64–65, 104–5;
and speculation, 102–8; and topology, 102

Speculation: and accumulation, 86–
87, 94–95, 98–99; as circulation of money, 86–89, 94–99,
133–34; definition of, 67–68,
97–98, 126; etymology of, 59,
73; and expansion in capitalism,
123–24, 129–30; and gam-
bling, 150–51, 154–55, 158;
and incest, 73–77; and interpretation, 59–60; logic of, 154–
63, 167–70; as melodrama, 80–
82; and narcissism, 59–65; and
naturalism, 71–72, 81, 163–64;
as parasitic activity, 145–46,
151; as process of abstraction,
68, 86, 89, 126–27, 142–43,
152–53, 164–65; in real estate,
61, 68–95; and secondary elaboration, 59–60; and space, 102–
5; in stock market, 125–65

Speculator: as actor, 78–80, 117; as
art dealer, 147–48; as author/
poet/artist, 72, 78–82, 92–93,
96, 116–17, 154; as gambler,
91–93, 98, 150, 154–55, 158;
as genius, 92; as master of signifiers, 69–71, 78–82; as parasite,
145–46, 151

State, Marxist theory of, 8–9, 29

Stock market, 71, 109; as arena of
abstraction, 131; corner on, 20,
93, 143, 160–63; history and
structure of, 148–52; mimesis
in, 140–41; psychology of,
140–42, 156; thematic representation of, 143–45

Stock shares: buying and selling of,
135; definition of, 128, 130–31;
and founding of the Banque
Universelle, 127–28; real estate
deeds as, 71; and universal signifier, 130–31; works of art as,
148

Symbolization, of money, 18, 21,
54

Symmetry: between Antoine and
Pierre Rougon, 12, 20; between
Bonapartism and republicanism,
11–12, 20; in *Au Bonheur des
Dames,* 98–99; between capitalism and socialism, 167–70; of
the *Rougon-Macquart* series, 44,
58; between Saccard and Busch,
166–70; between Saccard and
Gundermann, 166

Théry, Edmond, 149

Usurpation, 12–13, 21, 41. *See also*
Legitimacy; Pretender

Veblen, Thorstein, 122
Vial, André, 43

Weber, Samuel: *The Legend of Freud,*
59–61, 64

Zola, Emile: *L'Argent,* xi, 21, 28,
39, 43, 56–58, 73, 78, 89–91,
93, 95, 109, 124–71; *La Bête
humaine,* xii, 158; *Au Bonheur des
Dames,* 44, 57–58, 73, 78, 90,
95–125, 128–29, 133, 135, 140,
143, 145–46; *La Conquête de Plas-*

sans, 40–43, 58; *La Curée,* x, 19, 26, 57–97, 100, 105, 107, 109, 114, 119, 124–25, 128, 130, 133, 137, 143, 145, 154, 164; *La Débâcle,* x-xi, 21, 26–28, 32–33, 38, 58, 127, 165, 170; *Le Docteur Pascal,* 21; *La Fortune des Rougon,* 11–13, 43, 57, 108; *Germinal,* 43–56; *Nana,* 33–40, 44; *L'Oeuvre,* 146–48, 164; *Pot-Bouille,* 58; *Son Excellence Eugène Rougon,* x, 1–26, 28, 31, 33, 42–43, 87, 146; *Le Ventre de Paris,* 14, 43, 72

195